DAVE ALLEN

THE BIOGRAPHY

DAVE ALLEN
THE BIOGRAPHY

Carolyn Soutar

ORION

Copyright © Carolyn Soutar 2005

The right of Carolyn Soutar to be identified
as the author of this work has been asserted by her
in accordance with the Copyright, Designs and
Patents Act 1988.

First published in hardback in Great Britain in 2005 by
Orion Books
an imprint of the Orion Publishing Group Ltd
Orion House, 5 Upper St Martin's Lane,
London WC2H 9EA

1 3 5 7 9 10 8 6 4 2

A CIP catalogue record for this book is available
from the British Library.

ISBN: 0 75287 372 5

Printed in Great Britain by Mackays of Chatham plc, Chatham Kent

Every effort has been made to fulfil requirements
with regard to reproducing copyright material. The author
and publisher will be glad to rectify any omissions
at the earliest opportunity.

www.orionbooks.co.uk

CONTENTS

ACKNOWLEDGEMENTS

Dave Allen had friends around the world. Everywhere people wanted to share their memories of Dave: friends, television producers, staff and actors in the BBC, ITV and Australian television companies, theatre staff and promoters, members of the audience who had seen him perform, the 'family' of Butlins Redcoats and Dave's neighbours from Firhouse in Ireland. It has been one of the great pleasures of researching and writing this book to have heard their memories.

My thanks to: William Akers AM, Margaret Aitken, John Ammands, Roger Billington, Laurie Boynton, Ger Brady, Red Brigden, Jacqueline Clarke, Michael Condon, Patrick Condon, Simone Condon, Barry Cryer, Ian Davidson, Noel Delaney, Rosemary Delaney, Dr Oliver Double, Timmy Duggan, Paddy Egan, Jane Fletcher, Sabina Franklyn, Michael Freedland, Tony Goodliffe, Tony Guest, Geoff Harvey, Caroline Howard, Kerry Jewel, John Jordan, John Kennedy, Peter Laskie, Dizzie Leslie, Richard Lyle, the Hon. Russell Marshall CNZM, Rocky Mason, Ernest Maxim, Gerry Maxim, Bruce Menzies, James Moir, Richard Morris, John Moulton, Roger Myers, Lynda Noon, Cahill O'Shannon, Paddy O'Toole, Dee Piggott, Kenneth Pitt, André Ptaszynski, Juliet Ramsay, Tony Ramsay, Brian Robb,

Liz Scammell, Warren Seal, Michael Sharvell-Martin, Linda Sharvell-Martin, Patricia Smyllie, Max Tyler, Peter Vincent, Reece Warren, Peter Whitmore, Valerie Williams, Mary McNally and Pat O'Neill of Tallaght Historical Society, Alan Morgan of Terenure College Past Pupils' Union, Mick McKenna of Terenure Rugby Club, Sr Pat Shaffrey of St Mary's College Past Pupils' Union, Pat O'Mahony at Newbridge College, Rollercoaster Records, David Cotter and Kieran Swords of South Dublin County Council, the British Music Hall Society (Badger Press), the Butlins Archives, the Phil Warren Trust, NZ, Jim Davies at the British Airways Archives and Museum, Ralph Bott at the Sydney Opera House, Beverley Barnes at the Alhambra Theatre in Bradford, the Seymour Centre in Sydney, the Opera House in New Plymouth, NZ, the Grand Opera House in Belfast, the Hippodrome in Birmingham, the London Coliseum and the Dominion Theatre on Tottenham Court Road in London.

Various newspapers were also very generous with their assistance: *Ireland on Sunday*, the *Mail on Sunday*, the *Daily Mail*, the *Sunday Mirror*, the *Sunday Times*, the *Observer*, the *Churchill Press* in New Zealand, the *New Zealand Listener* and the *Sydney Morning Herald*.

I would also like to thank Wendy Wilders, Regina Lavelle in Eire, Cyril Jones in Australia and Christine Holland in New Zealand.

Thanks of course to the support and vision of my agent Peter Cox and the enthusiasm of Ian Marshall at Orion.

Carolyn Soutar
July 2005

PROLOGUE

————

THE BEST BLOKE ON TELEVISION
(CITY HALL, NEWCASTLE UPON TYNE 1988)

Dave Allen was holding a handbill that had been carefully preserved and framed; he looked bemused. His sparkling eyes were laughing over the top of half-moon glasses which were perched on the end of his nose. The famous jet-black thatch of hair was now a long grey mop and very windswept. He was wearing a much-worn grey pullover with holes at each elbow.

The handbill was from times past. He called me over to 'take a look at this'. The top of the bill was 'Britain's International Teen Singing Star' Helen Shapiro and down below her name was Dave Allen as compère. The eye-catching act was a group called the Beatles.

I saw that the date on the poster was 1963 and, without thinking, told Dave that I would have been nearly ten. He looked resignedly at me over the top of his glasses. As this was the legendary Dave Allen, the man who could make audiences weep with laughter at his sideways glance at the

English language, a man who could rant for twenty minutes about a sign that said 'Strawberries, Drive In' – 'Can't I drive in? I'm not a strawberry, but then I have never seen a strawberry drive' – and muse how someone could announce 'Ear-piercing while you wait' – 'Do you have many people who try to leave their ears with you, or anything else for that matter, while they go out shopping?' – I waited for his response. Dave Allen told me a story.

'This brings back memories. Helen Shapiro would have been just seventeen. I had been on tour with Helen for weeks and then we were joined by the Beatles. I changed from having my own slot on the show to being the compère.

'It was a very tough tour of one-night stands. It was a dreadful winter that year and we all froze. Helen and the guys travelled in a camper van. They were only just getting really well known. We were here in Newcastle in this room when John Lennon asked me how much their agent should be taking as a fee. He was really looking for some truth about all this. I told him ten to fifteen per cent tops. John looked horrified; he told me that Brian Epstein had been taking thirty per cent. They were just young guys who needed help.' 23 March 1963 dated the event precisely.

Take a glass of whisky, J&B of course, a missing finger, a tall leather bar chair, an acute, sometimes searingly accurate view of the absurdities of life, language, religion and sex, and you, along with millions of others, have conjured up the image of Gilbert David Tynan O'Mahony, known to all of us as Dave Allen. As this was 1988, there was no Gauloise cigarette; they had gone – 'Why should I pay someone else to kill me?' – but the rest was the same.

2

He was still the only person who could scream 'The Pope's a poof' at a 'shockproof' watch in front of an audience of millions and get away with it, just.

Dave Allen was the founder of stand-up comedy, a voyeur of life and raconteur and observer of all things ludicrous. On stage he screamed, shouted, swore and ranted. Some complained that he blasphemed, but he said that he never 'intended to offend'. Off stage he was a quiet, serious, seemingly shy man, until an eyebrow arched and the word 'prat' was spat out at someone or something stupid or irritating.

We were halfway through the tour of *An Evening with Dave Allen* at the City Hall in Newcastle. You could clearly see the mark on the wall where the precious handbill usually hung in this tired 'green room', backstage. We were standing on a red and purple swirl carpet, surrounded by boxes and the usual chaos of a load-in. It was anything but glamorous, but it was very welcoming.

As soon as Dave had arrived, one of the crew had taken the framed poster down and proudly passed it to him. They were pleased to see him and knew that they were in for nights of laughter.

The crew member told Dave that he had instructed a rock-and-roll tour manager who had arrived a few weeks earlier with eight wagons of equipment, lighting, sound, costumes and staging that he should learn from Dave Allen – 'All Dave has with him is a girl and a car.' I was that girl, on tour in 1988 with my own private comedian and bon vivant.

In the touring estate car was *the* chair, a large white carpet, luggage, Dave's suits, several boxes of programmes, two cases of champagne and the mandatory bottles of J&B. There would only be the two of us on the road for nearly six months, criss-crossing the country and staying either a week or just the night everywhere from Aberdeen to Plymouth, Norwich to Belfast for *An Evening with Dave Allen.* It was a very big tour and it was a sell-out.

I had met the icon of my childhood, this iconoclastic television star and comedian, only a few months earlier, in September 1988. I had received a phone call from a company that I had never worked for before called Pola Jones (who were promoting the show with Phil McIntyre). They were looking for a tour manager to go out with Dave Allen on his UK tour. I had just finished work on the arena version of Verdi's *Aida* at Earls Court with over seven hundred cast members. An exhilarating experience, but for a theatre company manager, it was incredibly frustrating as there was no way you could get to know anyone. It was an alien situation if you were used to doing a tour of just five dressing rooms before curtain up and listening to all the gossip and worries of the cast.

Now I was going to work with just one man. For once, it was from the ridiculous to the sublime. It doesn't matter how many stars you meet or work with, you are always nervous when you meet them for the first time. Dave Allen had been a television star for most of my life. He became part of mine and thousands of families' viewing habits in the UK with *Sunday Night at the London Palladium* or with *The Val Doonican Show.* Then came the many variations of his own show, when he started to do his own act, which would be broadcast to millions of people around the world. Like most people, I did not realise that his television career had started in Australia. By the time we met he had been on our screens for over twenty-five years.

We met for the first time in an office off Wardour Street in London. I hadn't expected someone so quiet, so serious. That was my first impression of him. Of course, he was much older than I remembered from the television shows in the seventies and early eighties. He was shorter than me, probably about five feet seven inches. He was in his omnipresent grey jumper. In hindsight, it was a ludicrous situation, just twenty minutes to meet someone that you are going to work with, be responsible for and get on with for weeks on end. It was like being interviewed for a six-month platonic blind date.

Dave was doing radio and press interviews on the phone in a back office, and I assumed that he would judge me on gut instinct alone in between calls. He was charming, we both smiled, shook hands, and it was over. I was about to go on the road as tour manager to Dave Allen.

I picked up Dave from his house off High Street Kensington a few days later. It was early morning, and we were on our way to get the train from Paddington to Bristol for the start of a short publicity tour. In the cab from my side of London to his I had concerns, of course. This day would be a good litmus test before the tour. The work didn't worry me, although it was years since I had actually lit a show – been responsible for the lighting – and now I was organising the lighting for this star. The old maxim that if you can't see someone then you can't hear them was scaring me a little.

From the moment we got on the train I began to see the other side of this observant comedian. During breakfast I listened to him directing the programme designer and saw his cartoons and beautiful paintings that were going to be included in the programme. There were some political cartoons and paintings depicting abstract relationships. It was going to be fascinating.

His fame was not in doubt, but I was not prepared for the respect or admiration that millions of ordinary people had for him. When I went to pay for the breakfasts that morning, the dining-car steward wouldn't take any money, point-blank refused it. 'Are you his wife?' he asked. I explained who I was, and with a wagging finger, he told me that Dave Allen was 'the best bloke on television. He doesn't pay for anything on this train. I won't take any money from Dave Allen. Please tell him that's what I think.' I wasn't going to argue, and Dave seemed bashfully flattered, as if it were the first time that had ever happened, which I didn't believe.

The publicity tour was a whistle-stop affair to Bristol, Liverpool and Manchester. Dave, as the polished professional, went from radio programme to television studio and behaved as if he knew all the people interviewing him as old friends. Even when we met faded celebrities, turned stars of local radio, reminding Dave, with a hint of desperation, about their hit single from twenty years back, he smiled through it all. It must have been exhausting going through the same questions each time: about his finger, what the show would be about, how much work it was, was he looking forward to it and when was he going to be on television again? It was a tour de force and his humour didn't change, although I saw that in private he was completely different.

To round off our day, on our return to Paddington there was a horrendous queue at the taxi rank. We stood looking at this Exodus-like mass of people. Suddenly the queue became irrelevant as two cabbies ran up to Dave and jostled to say that they would take him home. We didn't pay for that journey either.

After that there was only a week before we went on tour. A tremendous amount of work goes into a tour even with just one person. There is no such thing as a small show. The production office was busy finalising hotels, deals with the theatres and venues and producing a tour bible for Dave and I with all the names and numbers that we would need for the next few months. My tasks before we left included negotiating the release of his favourite black leather show chair from another company and to stock up on glasses, champagne and J&B.

The first date of the tour was in Manchester at the Palace Theatre. There are various types of tour. In the industry they are referred to as 'a number one' or 'a number two'. A number-one tour is usually a warm-up before a season in the West End in London. The touring theatres will be the big, famous venues, including Newcastle, Leeds, Birmingham, Bristol, Brighton, Richmond and Manchester. The Palace Theatre in Manchester is a huge venue, and for a one-man show to fill this for a whole week and for it to have been sold out weeks in advance was fantastic. It was a big première for everyone. It was also a big stage for a comic to get his act over to the audience from. Stand-ups prefer working in small venues, clubs and pubs because they can get good audience contact and feedback. To work on a thirty-yard-wide black platform looking into a black cavern and make contact with the audience needs special expertise and courage.

In Manchester the load-in (the arrival and building of the scenery) for this show took minutes rather than the usual hours as there was just me and the contents of the car. The crew who were waiting for me were welcoming and excited about the week ahead. I had been there many times before over the years, but this time, instead of stacks of scenery in the wings, there was just a pile of programmes in boxes. No rails of costumes, just a couple of suits that went into the number-one dressing room.

There was a surreal moment between myself and the chief electrician when we were sitting in the stalls checking the lighting states, colours and follow spots as all we were watching was a chair and a table on a large white carpet. The atmosphere was electric, expectant.

There is nothing like the feel of a theatre on the night of a première. You know that it is going to be a full house, and there is a buzz everywhere. Hushed voices are interrupted by the sound of bottles being stacked on the shelves in the bars. They were anticipating a good take at the bars during the interval that night. They would not be disappointed. The ushers had a briefing and were told the running times of the show, and you knew that they would listen to every word, every night and would laugh until they cried. They all loved Dave Allen.

The theatre manager asked me for boxes of programmes. He had a laugh at the cover. It was one of Dave's cartoons called 'Captain Flash' who was wearing a blindfold, revealing a toothy smile and holding open his cape; he was stark naked. It wasn't a pretty sight. It was not the usual type of programme.

I phoned the hotel to see that Dave had arrived safely. He had but was swapping rooms, a ritual I was soon to discover. He hated lifts and always insisted on being on the ground or first floor. He asked me to buy him some pancake make-up and a sponge as he had forgotten them, and I hurtled out into the hot late afternoon to the nearest theatrical supplier and arrived back at the theatre to find Dave in residence. The stage door keeper was quick to tell me that I had missed his arrival and looked at me as if I had been out skiving. There were cards to be taken to Dave's room, and I was anxious to talk to him about the opening sequence, the running time, how part one ended and finally to ask him how he was. I didn't know him well enough to spot if he was nervous, but I was.

Dave told me that it was all really straightforward as there were clear cues to follow and asked me about the lighting and the follow spots. I reassured him that I had followed the colours for the lighting that he had given me and that the follow spots were looking forward to it, in fact everyone was. Then came the bombshell.

He told me that I would have to walk on to the stage in a blackout (there would be no lights on) with a tray of drinks and put them on the table, then get back to the prompt corner, the stage manager's desk and start the show. This was news to me and I was absolutely terrified. 'You are joking,' I implored hopefully. He wasn't, but he was laughing. He said that he didn't like the drinks sitting there all that time and, anyway, the ice would melt.

I left the calm of the number-one dressing room and headed for the wide, open spaces of the black wings on the opposite prompt side, the right-hand side of the stage. I practised walking to the chair and back, the slippery silver tray balanced on my hand, with my eyes shut, trying not to think about full glasses of booze that could slip off and crash. I was not looking forward to this. It sounded so simple, but in front of 1200 people a slip-up could ruin the start of the show, although as Dave told me with a rather mischievous twinkle in his eyes, 'It might get a few laughs.' This didn't reassure me.

Dave joined me on stage to do a sound check, and I got my first taste of his act, that soft voice and his expert sound effects with just a microphone, and my adrenaline kicked in. The stalls were suddenly populated by groups of ushers and theatre staff gathering to get their first glimpse of the great television star, Dave Allen. He said, 'Good evening, Manchester' to them all, and they waved back to him. He asked them if they were all well and happy, and a chorus of 'Yes, thanks, Dave' came back to him from all round the auditorium. There was good humour all round.

After the sound check he thanked everyone and headed back to his extraordinary pink dressing room. He asked the theatre manager why it was pink, and the answer was that it was a request from Shirley Bassey who just liked her dressing rooms to be pink. I asked Dave what colour he would like his dressing rooms to be for the rest of the tour, and he just gave me that over-the-top-of-the-glasses look.

We ended up in a lot of pink dressing rooms on that tour and listened in fascination to the tales of comedy double acts on the road and their fixations with checking that neither had a larger dressing room than the other, even to the extent of getting out tape measures to be absolutely sure.

I went back on to the deserted stage. The working lights were on in the auditorium, and I turned on the working light on stage. The space instantly lost its life and magic and became a dead space.

Usually there are people everywhere backstage: cast rehearsing, crew walking around, visitors coming to see the star for the traditional good-luck wish for the first night. This night was unique; I was the only one backstage and would be waiting anxiously in the wings for a show I have never rehearsed or seen. There was only one performer and he was quietly getting ready in his dressing room. I was thinking about the tray and the glasses and then looking in dismay at the distance to the table on stage.

The theatre manager came through the pass door and asked me if he could 'open the house' and let the audience in. I asked the lighting guys to put up the walk-in lighting that highlights the chair and to put the houselights on to full and said, 'Yes, we're clear' to the manager.

Almost immediately the sound of laughter filled the theatre. It sounded like the audience for a pantomime – noisy, expectant – except that there were no children in for this show; these were excited adults. There were snatches of 'There's his chair' and 'No booze on there yet' as they sat looking at the familiar sight of the chair and stool, anticipating the arrival of Dave Allen.

The star dressing room was right by the prompt corner in this theatre. Dave opened the door and asked me if I would mind ironing his shirt for him as he had brought one in that he wanted to wear, then he asked if I was all right and whether I knew what I was doing. With anyone else this would have appeared to be a loaded question, coming from Dave, though, it was a genuine concern for a colleague. I told him that I was fine, and he poured me a glass of champagne as I stood ironing his shirt.

Having a glass of champagne went against everything you usually do backstage when you are working. There are rules that state no alcohol on stage, none consumed in the wings or in any of the crew rooms, and I was certain that me versus a tray of drinks would not necessarily be helped with champagne inside me. But I took the glass and told myself that Dutch courage is a wonderful thing. Dave was sitting putting on his pancake make-up in the strange pink boudoir.

The promoters arrived at his dressing room and came in to wish him luck. All of a sudden the room was crowded out with well-wishers. They asked me if I had 'cracked the lighting'. I hoped that I had. Everyone was laughing and full of that nervous bonhomie which precedes an important event that must be left in the hands of just one person. They talked about Victoria Wood, who was out on the road at the same time; we were following her everywhere – 'At least you don't have a white grand piano to deal with.' We were following Billy Connolly around as well. We were in stellar company. They all laughed and, with cries of 'Break a leg!', left. I went back to my ironing board.

Dave passed me a bright-red silk pocket handkerchief to

iron, and as I turned to pick up the iron, I managed to throw the entire contents of my glass of champagne over it. I was horrified. He called me a 'dickhead' and roared with laughter. I was trying to dry it with the iron, and he said to forget it. It was like an Abbott and Costello routine in a dressing room. Dave stuffed the wet, champagne-soaked handkerchief in his top pocket and laughed at me. I returned to the stage and the sanctuary of the prompt corner. It was nearly time to start.

Dave came out of his dressing room and, with a quick 'Is my tie straight?' and thankfully no mention of that handkerchief, he headed off on the long walk round the back of the stage to the prompt, on the left-hand side. With our small 'set', we used just a quarter of this vast performance space. The walk round the back and past the huge pillars under the wooden dock doors set high off the ground was a long, lonely one. As I watched him I knew that unlike other shows there would be no one to greet him on the other side; he was on his own. I have no idea what that would feel like, whether you clear your mind of everything and focus, or go over the start of the show in your mind, listening to the buzz of the audience. The wait must feel endless.

The theatre manager came round to give me the clearance to start the show. He said that everyone was in and it seemed like a good crowd. They had done 'flying sales' with the programmes. I was not surprised. They were very unusual. I waved at Dave across the stage to signal that we were ready, and he gave me the thumbs up.

I checked that the follow-spot operators were ready to pick Dave up from mid-stage left and asked for the houselights out. Holding the tray with the drinks, I closed my eyes in preparation for a pitch-black stage and started my journey to the table in total darkness. This was a huge task for me as there hadn't been a lot of call for me to do this as a stage manager in opera and ballet. As I walked on to the stage I was greeted with wolf whistles. Horrified, I put the tray down quickly on the table and scuttled off in confusion.

Once safely in the prompt corner, I grabbed the headset and watched as Dave entered from stage left to be picked up by the follow spots. Dave Allen walked on to the stage and went straight to the microphone. The audience was applauding, and he said good evening and thanked them but asked why they were clapping as it wasn't that difficult to walk thirty feet from 'there to here'. They roared with laughter, and Dave continued, 'In case you wonder what I do, I tend to stroll around and chat. I'd be grateful if you would refrain from doing the same.' The irreverent Dave Allen was with them, and what was to be a highly successful tour had begun.

Dave told stories about age, of his frustration with the hair on his head, the skin on his hands and how memory deserts you with the onset of age. It was hysterical. Punctuated with passionate swearing, which surprised me, you could feel the audience agreeing with him and relaxing. I was laughing as much as the audience. It was a very physical performance, which I also hadn't expected.

When I had watched him on television, he had seemed contained and restrained on a small television screen. But here was a powerful performer acting his feelings; this wasn't a comic telling a tale. The ranting and pure rage filled the stage, and then quickly he brought it all back to himself by picking up a glass, looking at his watch, taking a few steps towards the wings or smoothing down his wild hair. I saw that the white carpet was a tool not only to help the audience focus on one person on an enormous stage but to give Dave a performance area and some boundaries. The act was explosive yet with acute timing and awareness of the audience's reaction.

Over the weeks ahead, I would see subtle changes to the routine reflecting where we were, what was in the news, the people we had watched after the show at meals and the feedback that he was getting from the audience. It was continually evolving, and it was mesmerising.

At the end of part one, he called to me from the stage and asked for the houselights up. He asked for a volunteer from the audience to make sure that they all get back in time. It would always be someone in the front row, and at first they looked doubtful, as if they were going to be made a fool of, but he would never do that. He asked his victim to 'Get everyone back here in, what do you think, twenty minutes? Can you do that? Great. See you back here, then.'

Dave left the stage, and the audience laughed as they gradually realised that he really had gone and they now had an empty stage in front of them. It took them a few seconds to understand that they should leave, and they headed for the bars.

I told him that it was 'great stuff'. I meant it, as I hadn't heard the act before and it was a unique experience for me working on something so funny with so much feedback from the audience. He looked really pleased that I had liked it. He had the ability to look astonished when anyone praised him.

The next few weeks took on a whole new aspect, as I knew that I would be laughing most of the time. It was a very special way to earn a living, being entertained like this each day.

The front-of-house manager came round to see me as there had been a complaint about the language. It was a predictable situation as it stated clearly on all the publicity that this was an 'adult' show. I believed it was an attempt to get a refund. I asked the manager what he usually did in this situation and told him that my instinct would be to remind the person about the word 'adult' and to either stay or leave but don't complain. He agreed and left to take on the challenge of the complainer.

Towards the end of the interval I collected the champagne from the fridge in Dave's dressing room as he would need it on stage at the top of part two. I took advantage of the fire curtain (the 'iron') being in to sneak the drinks on to the table. I didn't want to chance my luck twice on the first evening.

When we got clearance that all the audience were back in and with the 'iron' safely out, Dave walked on to the stage and handed a glass of champagne to the leader of the audience from the very front of the stage, in gratitude for getting all the audience back on time from the bars. It was a nice moment. Dave asked his 'victim' if the lady beside him was his wife. Inevitably they replied that she wasn't, and before they could explain, Dave had countered with, 'Does your wife know you are out with a strange woman?' He offered the now highly embarrassed woman a glass of champagne, and when she tried to take it from Dave, he hung on to it. Everyone was laughing at the poor woman. Dave finally let it go with a ribald remark about her grip and it probably explaining why they had no children. The ice was broken for part two and we were off on a whirlwind about the death trap that is cling film. – 'Can anyone explain to me how a metre-wide piece of cling film can reduce itself to the size of a piece of old chewing gum? When I start out, I pull it off the roll, turn to the sandwich I have left on the side ready to be wrapped, and in the process of turning round, this carefully selected piece of cling film has wrapped itself around my arm and is completely unusable. I turn back to get another piece but now cannot get rid of this stuff that has attached itself to my hand, so I go back to the roll of cling film and start again' – and on and on he takes us around the kitchen and how someone could invent something which is actually unusable.

His children became the focus of this section on communication and the day-to-day frustrations of dirty rings around the bath – 'That no one has left because no one has had a bath' – the mystery of how no one else replaces lavatory paper in his house except him and the ultimate frustration at finding one tiny piece of paper left on the roll. 'When I ask either of my children who was the last to use the bath or the lavatory, they both deny it. Mr Fucking Nobody lives in our house.' I idly wondered how our complainer was doing at this point in the show.

'Now, the telephone in my house is on the ground floor. When I get to the phone, I answer it, and a completely

incoherent voice on the other end says, "Is Nerner there?"'
A full five minutes later, following trips up- and downstairs
and back to the phone, we discover that 'Nerner' is Edward.
This telephone sequence has the audience roaring with
laughter.

You could hear that the audience were carefully balanced
between wincing at how close to reality all the stories were
and hysteria all through the show. Then we went back in
time to his childhood. I was still laughing with the audience. But now there is a darkness to the stories about his
childhood. He told of priests swooping around the dormitories, 'scaring the shit' out of the children, arms flailing
around with descriptions of black cloaks like wings. While
most of the show was projected out to the audience, involving them and saying, 'We have all done this, haven't we?'
the childhood ones were turned off stage, towards the
wings, inwards and not for sharing. We were hearing all
about 'God's storm troopers' and the 'SS in drag', the priests.

He stopped the priest sketch from becoming a nightmar-
ish image and the risk of losing the audience by turning it
on a sixpence. It became a joke about 'God walks in myste-
rious ways' and with Dave aping a strange Monty Python-
esque walk across the stage.

Then Dave took us into the other side of his childhood
and his family life as he was growing up. There was a tale
about one of his aunts and how she powdered her face so
much that she left half-moons of powder all over it. He tells
the audience how he was pressed up against her vast bosom
and this violet-smelling women told him to 'Give your aunt
a great big kiss' and the clouds of powder that flew up. The

story reminded me of one of his paintings in the programme of a small boy clinging to a vast white expanse of apron. You could not see the mother's face as she didn't exist above her chest. I had asked him if it was a child clinging to his mother because he is scared. Dave had told me that it was a child desperate for attention and for love.

Then we were off driving with him, calling himself, like everyone else of course, the best driver in the world. He wondered why it was that when you 'make a mistake when driving or notice that someone else has, that they sit looking straight forward, pretending that they are so perfect that nothing has happened'. How he ended up calling every other driver 'stupid bastard, look there's another bastard, you fat bastard'. Then a description of what happens when he lets people out in front of him and they don't say 'thank you' so he decides that he won't let anyone out into the road in front of him for miles to make them pay for someone else's failings. How his car told him when he was running out of petrol, bleating 'petrol, petrol' for hours on end.

His fear of lifts came next and the horror of travelling in a lift in Canada that goes up to the fifty-fourth floor. By the time it arrives at the top floor, he is grovelling on the floor in terror and screams when the lift stops, as he knows that it has stuck and he is trapped, only to realise that the door behind him has opened. It is very clever, especially when you realise that it is based on his real fear of lifts and that he has developed it into a fast-moving episode that has everyone screaming with laughter with him, but living every moment of the fear.

To end the show Dave told the story of the bizarre way we

teach children to tell the time. Looming over an invisible small child in front of him, he started by calmly describing how it was 'very important to learn to tell the time'.

'Why, Daddy?' said Dave, impersonating the invisible child.

'You need to be able to tell the time in order to get to work on time.'

'But, Daddy, I don't go to work.'

'Don't be stupid. Shut up and listen.'

And we are off on how 'three' and 'nine' could be 'fifteen', 'forty-five' or a 'quarter' and 'sometimes even three-quarters'. That 'one' can be 'five' and 'two', 'ten'.

'What time is it when the little hand is at twelve and the big hand is at two? What do you mean you don't know? Haven't you been listening? It is so simple. Don't cry, you are not trying,' he admonished the invisible child.

By the time he started to tell the child how 'eight' can be 'twenty' or 'forty', depending, how 'seven' and 'five' can be 'twenty-five' and 'thirty-five' as well, the story was full of rage and frustration.

The completely befuddled, tearful child ends up being thwacked round the ear, with a loud 'thdunk' on the microphone, for not understanding and for 'being so stupid'. It resonated with the whole audience either from the frustration of being the child or the exasperation of being the parent. The end of the sketch was done at break-neck speed, switching between the child and Dave, and the audience was near hysteria and exhausted.

It was the end of the show, and Dave left the stage with the farewell line 'May whatever God you support, go with you wherever you go.' There was a fun bit of business with a follow spot that he told to stay on the carpet and then he returned to collect a drink, to much laughter. Clutching his drink, he left for the first of many curtain calls. The audience didn't want to lose him. The first night of the tour was a success.

Dave made his way round from the prompt side of the stage and was smiling hesitantly. He should have been delighted, but he was looking for reassurance from the small group of promoters and friends waiting to see him. There was a great feeling backstage. Even though the tour was a sell-out, the word-of-mouth on just how good Dave Allen was would spread along all the theatres that we were due to visit. There would have been a healthy expectation for everyone working at the theatres even before the press had written their reviews.

The number-one dressing room was swamped with people as congratulations were shared all round. Dave handed round some more glasses and rescued me by asking me to check the restaurant for that night. On my return to the celebrations, the promoter told me that I 'had done a great job with the lighting'. I had had enough of the lighting fixation and was still recovering from being wolf-whistled.

We all departed a few minutes later for the restaurant in Manchester's Chinatown. On the way out of the theatre to the taxis Dave grabbed my arm to whisper to me 'Was I okay?' I nodded and smiled back to him. Even though he was the star and by rights should be the centre of attention, he was watching out for everyone else. I learned later that he hated the 'showbiz' side of the profession and all that 'crap', and he hated anyone who was a 'star'.

The meal was a good celebration and the first of many Chinese meals taken late at night and running into the early morning. Some would be with groups of Dave's friends from his club days; on the whole there would just be the two of us, watching other diners and talking about life, politics and our own lives. At the end of the meal there were good wishes for the tour and jokes and laughter. Then there was just the two of us heading back to our hotel.

The receptionist at the hotel was waiting for us and apologetic as the local paper had run a story about Dave being allergic to pillows and lifts. Dave shrugged and headed for his room. I decided that all publicity was good publicity and told her not to worry.

The next day was the start of our touring routine. I collected the local papers and checked for the reviews. We had been a little late the night before for some of them to have included reviews, but there were a couple and they were great. I phoned the theatre to share the good news with the press office, and they said that they were delighted. Dave had asked me to find a swimming pool, and we found one not too far from the hotel with a spectacular stained-glass roof and the essential sauna. As I left the pool to negotiate a deal for him for the week, I caught a glimpse of a group of people surrounding Dave in the shallow end of the pool. There was a lot of laughter and bobbing heads. They all moved from the pool to a spa bath and their private audience with Dave Allen continued. I waved to Dave as a signal to see if he needed rescuing. He didn't. He was with 'normal' people, listening and talking.

At the theatre the cleaners and ushers said how much they had enjoyed the show and asked whether I knew if he did the same thing every night. I told them that I was sure that it would have lots of changes, and they said that they couldn't wait.

In the office I looked through the tour book at all the places coming up, the 'one-nighters' at Brighton and Reading, the rest or travel days and the long stays at Belfast, Aberdeen, Edinburgh and Glasgow, then the long, seemingly illogical journeys from Nottingham to Belfast and back to Norwich. I was looking forward to Belfast with Dave Allen. I had never been there, and I knew we would be welcomed and have a great time. It was an exciting prospect.

On the second night there were just the two of us in another Chinese restaurant. We sat and talked, and he asked me about my life and my career. We discovered that there were some intriguing links and coincidences. We had lived in the same block of flats, Gilray House in Lancaster Gate, in 1960. My parents and I had lived on the top floor, and Dave two stairwells along, again on the top floor, with superb views over Kensington Gardens. I would have been about six or seven when he was coping with a girlfriend 'who tried to throw herself off the roof'. I don't remember any of this, of course, but my parents did. At that time it was just an incident at the flats, as Dave Allen was unknown to most of us in England.

There was a strange little bohemian enclave that lived in these flats at the time. In addition to Dave Allen, there was Donald Houston, our old neighbour from Talgarth Mansions at Barons Court and the star of *The Blue Lagoon*, Joe Loss, the band leader, and many others who had all been forced out of their homes in Barons Court to make way for the Cromwell Road extension. With the show-business columnist Donald Zec and the up-and-coming chat-show host Eamonn Andrews in Maitland Court opposite, it was a unique corner of London.

After that first link we should not have been surprised when our conversation drifted round to my father, who had worked at the *Daily Mirror*, and I discovered that he worked with Dave's then ex-brother-in-law, Richard Stott. The six degrees of separation rule appeared to be working well between us.

I told Dave that I had actually first met him in 1973 at the London Coliseum. I had just joined the then Sadler's Wells Opera as an assistant stage manager and *Peter Pan* was mostly a matinee show running each day before we changed for the opera performance at night.

I was just nineteen when I came face to face with Captain Hook, also known as Dave Allen. He was struggling outside the stage-management office with a not very surreptitious cigarette, moustache, beard, tricorn hat, lace cuffs, sword and a hook. He asked me if I could try and sort out the mess for him, which I did. I thought that he was flirting outrageously, and I remember telling everyone else back in the stage-management office that I had actually spoken to *the* Dave Allen.

Back in Manchester we sat and watched the other diners and we started to invent stories about the other couples and groups eating. Over the weeks these invented stories slowly appeared in his act. It was fascinating. Dave told me about his experiences in Australia, how he developed his routine and how he had started. He told me about his girlfriend, Karin Stark, who was working in the offices of a theatre producer, and that he hoped she would be coming out to visit him. He was very proud of his two children: Edward who was at university and Jane who was at Mountview Theatre School, training to be a stage manager.

I was beginning to understand that, just like all of us with a work life and a private life, he was two distinct people. There was the comedian, perfectly turned out in his immaculate suits, thrilling millions of people with his humour and timing, doing his job. Then there was the off-duty Dave Allen, not giving a stuff about what he wore or what people thought and really rather uncommunicative when he wanted to be. He shut himself away on off-duty days and hid with his work, his painting or talking to his family.

I also discovered about his generosity and, like all the other people I would speak to who had worked with him or for him, that paying for meals was impossible and that this meal in Manchester would be the first of many meals that he would refuse to let me pay for. Even when verging on an argument about it many weeks later in Glasgow, rather than have a public row about this in a restaurant, I surrendered and lost.

The highlight of our off-duty time in Manchester was a trip to the art gallery in Salford that at that time housed all of L.S. Lowry's paintings. Dave had asked me to see when we could go. He was very interested in L.S. Lowry and because of his love of painting wanted to see the collection. As if by magic the name Dave Allen opened up storage racks in vaults that the public don't usually see.

Downstairs, underneath the gallery, we pulled out row upon row of sliding racks holding four or six paintings in each rack and each painting in turn worth hundreds of thousands of pounds. The curator told us the story of a rent collector with his extraordinary talent for creating his matchstick people and capturing snapshots of industrial England. Dave asked about Lowry's family and the curator told us about a daughter, I think, who was a recluse and didn't like being approached by anyone. I think that Dave had hoped that he would be able to meet her or any other descendants. The pictures we saw were wonderful, and Dave told me how he had started drawing as a child and liked to do everything from cartoons, political satire and drawings of animals or wildlife to his impressionist paintings that were in the pointillist style. It was a natural extension of his observational style as a comic to take it off stage and produce it in his art work.

On the last night in Manchester Dave asked me to invite everyone on the crew who had helped – the follow-spot operators, sound, lighting and anyone else who had helped us – to his dressing room for a drink after the last curtain. Very few professionals do this nowadays. It is a throwback to the days of variety, where there were various 'hanging offences' lurking for unsuspecting performers: failing to tip the right people, failing to be polite to the stage manager, the stage door keeper and the theatre manager. Any of these could result in never having another booking at that theatre. Dave Allen meticulously checked that he had the right names on the envelopes for tips and that we hadn't forgotten anyone.

After the show he welcomed his guests into his room to thank them personally. Clutching their glasses of champagne, some of them with a painfully shy girlfriend in tow, they stood and joked with Dave. They unanimously said how much they had enjoyed the show and how much they had laughed.

The follow-spot operators complained that they had been shaking so much with laughter, with tears streaming down their faces, that it had been impossible to do their work on some nights. The cassettes that the sound guys had carefully recorded of the shows and which Dave used to check his timings were solemnly handed over.

As the crew handed back their glasses, they presented us with a small package each. We had arrived at the theatre one evening to hear the sounds of Clannard being played by the sound department. It was the first time that either of us had heard this haunting music, and they had thoughtfully got us copies to play in our cars on the long journeys ahead. This last-night party was a routine that would occur everywhere and earned Dave the reputation of being 'a true gentleman and professional' at all the theatres or venues that we visited.

On tour with Dave Allen will always be the job that I remember as having been fun. Even when I was trying unsuccessfully to find bottles of J&B and Moët & Chandon in the backstreets of Nottingham and running out of time, or being lectured by an extremely irritable Dave Allen on the state of his suits and what a local dry-cleaner had done to them, it was always fun.

There are some jobs that get omitted from my 'CV'; they

were critical disasters, short runs or shows that no one could stand or are too many years ago. I have always kept this tour on mine. Everyone spots the name Dave Allen and asks me about the job and him. Just reading the name Dave Allen makes people smile.

This book is about the life and career of Dave Allen, 'a true gentleman' and 'the best bloke on television'.

CHAPTER ONE

TARZAN AND THE
HALF-CROWN FUTURE

In May 1941 Dublin, the capital of neutral Eire, was hit by two bombs. The first hit the city itself. The fact that it was a mistake by the Luftwaffe did not help the people who lived on the North Strand where several houses were destroyed. The second mistake fell in Terenure, a suburb of Dublin, not far from Knocklyon. This bomb hit an aerodrome that had been built on a field that Dave Allen's great-grandfather had sold to the British for development, much to the outrage of his daughter, Dave Allen's great-aunt, Katharine Tynan.

The beautiful city of Dublin has been a city of conflict intellectually and politically for centuries, finally achieving Home Rule following the signing of the Anglo–Irish Treaty on 6 December 1921 and the formation of the Irish Free State on January 1922, but at great cost with civil war and death to hundreds of people on both sides.

With certain areas of the city ghetto-like for the

Protestant and Roman Catholic communities alike, money also caused rifts and difficulties within the city for centuries either through famine, strife or bad luck. Pre-war Dublin was a tough place; the gap between families that had money or were on the breadline was vast, even before the war started. The financial hardships of Dave Allen's childhood paralleled those of James Joyce, whose parents fell on hard times. (Joyce was removed from his expensive boarding school with the fees unpaid, and his parents left their substantial home and moved across to the unfashionable Northside and into a tiny flat.) Dave's childhood was also marked by tragedy; he learned to be a watcher and a listener, someone who could mix with anyone from any background. At school he became a defender of the underdog, something that would stay with him all his life.

Gilbert David Tynan O'Mahony, or Dave Allen, was born on 6 July 1936 to Jean, an English nurse, and Gerard John Cullen Tynan O'Mahony, managing editor of the *Irish Times*. David was the youngest with two brothers, John and Peter. To the casual observer David Tynan O'Mahony had all the trappings of privilege. He was also part of a creative, artistic and intelligent family.

The Tynan O'Mahonys had an impressive family tree, one which boasted novelist, author and poetess Katharine and, her younger sister, writer and journalist Nora. It was Dave Allen's great aunt Katharine who was the first to make her mark on the literary world, producing her first opus, a book of verse, at age seventeen and becoming a member of the cultural nationalist organisation, the Irish Literary Movement. Katharine became friends with W.B. Yeats, who later visited her at Whitehall, and with John Butler Yeats, who painted her portrait.

Great aunt Katharine wasn't just a literary prodigy; she was way ahead of her time politically. Not only a staunch campaigner against the plight of shop girls and single mothers, she was also a loud voice against capital punishment. Ambitious and adventurous, her campaigning took her out of Dublin. She took part in the charge for universal suffrage and attended the World Congress of Women in Rome in 1914.

Like many middle-class people of the time, Katharine's own politics were quite complicated. She had close relationships with members of the ascendancy, notably Lady Aberdeen and Lady Fingal, but she was also a supporter of Home Rule.

Her father's decision to sell some of his land to the British, which was subsequently developed as the aerodrome that would be bombed all those years later, was incomprehensible to her. It was to him she wrote the poem 'The Aerodrome', documenting the 'defilement' of their land by the British after the airstrip was completed.

Katharine's younger sister, Nora, had ambitions too. Nora edited the *Freeman's Journal* as well as contributing articles for the *Irish Monthly*. Although, it seems, she did look up somewhat to her older sister; while Katharine kept her maiden name out of reverence to her father, Andrew Cullen Tynan, Nora apparently kept her maiden name in order that she would continue to be recognised as Katharine's sister.

In 1895 Nora married John O'Mahony, a barrister, and moved to Airfield Cottage in the village of Tallaght, and in April 1900 Gerard John Cullen Tynan O'Mahony, Dave Allen's father, was born. His grandparents' marriage was to be short-lived, however, since John died of heart disease less than a decade later in 1904, when he was only thirty-four. Their youngest, Barry, was a lawyer. By all accounts Barry Tynan O'Mahony was something of a character. A man who 'was fond of a jar', Barry would take cases from locals who couldn't afford legal representation. In exchange for a few drinks, Barry would see them through the courts. A bachelor, he died two years before his elder brother, Gerard John Cullen Tynan O'Mahony, Dave Allen's father.

Neighbours said that Gerard, or Cullen as he was known, served in the Great War (the First World War) and on his safe return he went into the *Irish Times* as a typesetter. He was ambitious and quick from the outset. In spite of his rapid progression through the ranks of this prestigious paper, however, his time there was marked by a dreadful accident, which occurred in the lift at the newspaper's offices. His foot was trapped so badly that the only way to free himself and save his life was to amputate his own foot, which he did. Cullen was left with an artificial foot made from cork and, consequently, a nickname, 'Corky'.

Jean Archer was the nurse who tended to his wound and later became his wife. Dave's father, Corky, was a very talented man, extremely funny, a comic, a mimic and a talented artist. Dave Allen inherited all these talents. He was to regret his whole life that his father never lived to see him as an adult.

Jean Archer and G.J.C. Tynan O'Mahony's first child, Peter Tynan O'Mahony, was born in 1930. The family was living in an apartment in Merrion House, Lower Fitzwilliam Street, Dublin. This house formed part of a terrace of tall, elegant, four-storey Georgian houses built by Lord Fitzwilliam on Dublin's Southside. Their second son, John, was born shortly after, and their youngest child, Gilbert (David), spent the first four years of his life there.

In 1940 they moved into Cherryfield, a large house near to the old family home at Knocklyon. In the early forties it was a beautiful rural suburb some twelve miles from Dublin. There was nothing but fields and houses, and the houses were large enough to have their own gatehouses. It was definitely where the more affluent Dubliners lived. Cherryfield was built on the site of an older house called Cherrytree, which dated back to before 1730. The original house was partially rebuilt and extended into Cherryfield, a substantial house with 'wings', the architectural description of which reads 'a two-storey, three-bay house with a projecting Ionic porch and unusual tripartite windows'.

The O'Mahonys shared the large Cherryfield house with the Delaney family. The Delaneys, who worked for a major tobacco firm, were considered to be substantially more 'sophisticated' still than the O'Mahonys. The Delaneys lived in the front of the house, while the O'Mahonys lived in a wing at the back.

When Dave Allen was growing up, the Knocklyon and Firhouse area had little in common with the modern suburb it is today. During the sixties many of the beautiful Georgian terraces in Dublin, along with the city slums, were demolished to make way for modernisation. As the city expanded, the Knocklyon and Firhouse area was transformed by dual carriageways and flyovers.

The Tynan O'Mahonys' home, Cherryfield, had a great view over the Dodder River and back towards the Dublin mountains. The setting was impressive with over eighty acres of land, but like many rural areas at the time, there was no running water. Templeogue was the nearest village with a sole shop, but Firhouse and Tallaght were nearby.

Paddy O'Toole, a neighbour and friend of Dave and his brothers, remembers their childhood: 'We used to cross the river by stepping stones back then. All of us went trout catching and swimming in the river. When the weather was bad, we were in each others house playing Monopoly.

'It was real country round here back then. Templeogue village only had one shop, so all of us boys would be sent on errands by our mothers. Dave, Johnny and I were always getting water from the wells for the houses.

'We would take the dogs off rabbiting in the fields. Dave and Johnny had a big collie dog, Bruce. Johnny had a smaller dog too, Tuppence, that he had rescued. It had gone down the waterfall at Templeogue bridge and couldn't get out, so he jumped in and saved it. That was the type that John was. Peter was older, and he was good at cricket and rugby.

'Dave was always very pale and quiet. He had the poshest accent of the three of them. Dave was always telling stories, but they were all pranksters. They used to swing mangels [beets] out of the trees at people going by, and at Halloween they hollowed out the mangels, stuck candles in them and put them in the trees to scare everyone. Then they had the trick of leaving a wallet stuffed with grass on the road for someone to pick up. They were always up to something.

'John was always taking off the Three Stooges, and Dave would sit and watch his older brother. He was like all younger brothers, watching and following the big boys. We did a bit of entertaining as well. There was an outshed at the back of Cherryfield, and we put on a play – *Murder in the Red Barn*. All of us were in it: Peter, John, David, some of the Clarkes [the sons of the well-known poet Austin Clarke]. The Clarkes lived at Bridge House. It poured with rain that day, and there wasn't a big audience, a lot of hens, though, but we had fun.'

The family had made lots of friends in Firhouse, and all of the locals remember the Tynan O'Mahonys. Mary McNally's brother went to Terenure College in 1939. His classmate was Johnny O'Mahony, Dave's brother. Mary remembers the three-year-old Dave on a sports day in 1939: 'We were standing in the crowd and I felt this push against my leg and there was this little boy running in and out between people and pushing against people. I asked my brother who he was, and he said, "Oh, that's Gilbert Tynan O'Mahony, the little pest." People called Dave "Gilbert" when he was young. I remember joking about it with Peter afterwards. Dave didn't lose that mischief when he got older either. I remember Dave and Peter sitting up on the high wall beside the house pegging pine cones at the people passing underneath. They got up to everything.'

The local pub, Delaney's (now the Knocklyon Inn), was right next door to Cherryfield and was a family-run inn. The Tynan O'Mahonys and all the families went to Delaney's each day. Like many pubs it was the hub of village life, and everyone remembers the Tynan O'Mahonys and the young Dave, especially his ability to sit still and watch people, absorbing everything they did and said. It was also when he started drawing.

Rosemary Delaney remembers, 'David used to sit listening to the farmers drinking at the bar. They all thought he was a friendly little boy. When my husband was bottling the Guinness and ale out the back, which we did back then, he would look round and there would be young David hovering at the doorway watching him using the bottling machine.'

Lena Delaney used to give Dave a small glass of stout in a whisky glass. 'Everyone remembers him as a quiet lad, with a dark shock of hair, his fringe pulled to the side, sitting and listening to the farmers talking about their cattle, the sheep auctions, the tall tales and stories.'

Dave Allen was sent to Firhouse National School when he was four. Noel Delaney used to walk the young Dave to school at the request of Corky, Dave's father. 'His father asked me to look after him and walk him the one mile or so to the school. Corky was a nice, quiet man and a fairly big man. He would have a few drinks in the pub. His wife was a tall, slender, friendly woman. She was pretty good-looking too. No one ever had a bad word to say about the Tynan O'Mahonys in the bar.'

A picture drawn by nine-year-old David of his father having a drink, with an intriguing patch over his eye, hangs in the bar in Delaney's, given to the owners by Peter Tynan O'Mahony.

Dave's childhood evenings after school were spent playing

football with his friends, although they all say that he was-n't that good. In 1941, when the bomb was dropped on the aerodrome, the Tynan O'Mahonys moved out to Keenagh, a small village outside the town of Longford and almost in the centre of the country. Neighbours said that it really rattled the O'Mahonys, in a sense scaring them away, and the mother and the three boys moved out for eighteen months. The bombings had been a shock to the whole of Dublin, and a lot of families took stock of what they should do with their families, in case it happened again. Dave's father, Corky, stayed on at the *Irish Times*. Dave always described his father in later years as 'a cuddler'. The young Dave Tynan O'Mahony would miss his father for this short time apart.

Vacant houses in the country had been earmarked before the war, and the Tynan O'Mahonys were installed in the Miller's Cottage (also known as the Seven Dwarfs' Cottage because of all the work that was done there). The cottage was part of the picturesque estate, with a large house, called Mosstown, at Keenagh.

At that time Mosstown had its own private driveway, a canal and acres of land and would have been a fairly presti-gious address and is the only house to have survived in its original form. The cottage faced the old mill, which was burned around the turn of the century, but the rusting machinery remains in front of the shell of the old building.

Keenagh was different from the usual isolated rural town. Instead of being staunchly Catholic and insular, there was a mix of people, a hangover from the plantations. There was also a military base nearby, and families from all over the country had been moved there before the war. When the Tynan O'Mahony family came to live there, they would not have felt unduly uncomfortable, other than because they were from the big city, Dublin.

Dave Tynan O'Mahony started at Keenagh National School in June 1941, at the age of four years and eleven months. Paddy Egan started school on the same day as David and sat beside him in school. Paddy is a local historian and community worker and has vivid recollections of sitting beside David O'Mahony on their first day at school. 'I remember David was very bright. He was able to write and we weren't. We were all impressed by that. We started school on the same day, and there was only four days' difference in our ages. That's why I knew him that little bit better and because I sat beside him. That was great for both of us because you'd be worried you would be put sitting beside a girl. For us then there was nothing worse than having to sit beside a girl.

'David always wore a very distinctive little brown check suit. He was always well dressed, whereas you'd see children wearing raggedy old torn trousers and maybe no boots. He always had that very remarkable mop of hair that was swept to one side. The family seemed very comfortable.'

Dave and his brothers, like thousands of evacuees all over England and Ireland, found themselves in a strange environment, having to cope, having to fit in. Unlike most evacuees, though, they had their mother with them and had not been farmed out to families miles away from their hometown. It was a wrench for the small boys to be away from their father, and Dave's mother was anxious about Corky being on his own, spending his days at work and evenings drinking in Delaney's and potentially in danger from more bombing raids, or mistakes, in Dublin.

With his 'posh' Dublin accent, talent for comedy, a knowledge of chimpanzees and zoos that none of the other children had, Dave Tynan O'Mahony was the centre of attention. Paddy, his school friend continued, 'Dave wasn't troublesome, but he was more of the gnat. He was more of the entertainer, and even at six he was an extrovert. He was very good at making friends. He entertained the teacher and the whole school.

'The teacher would get him up, and he'd behave like a monkey. He had the advantage over all of us because he had been born in Dublin. None of us had ever been in Dublin or to the zoo. He'd impersonate a chimpanzee, go through all the motions – scratching underneath his arms, jumping from one desk to the other – and it was great sport at that time for all of us.

'The teacher had a great rapport with him. We were a little jealous that she liked him so much. As very small children the teacher would bring an odd one up and put them on her knee, and she had a great thing with the five year old David O'Mahony. I remember him out in the schoolyard too. There were a few lads from Dublin in the school around that time. There was one lad who had a very strong Dublin accent. I often wondered since if we were kind of bullying him in a way. We'd get around him and imitate his Dublin accent. Children can be very hard at that age.

'But Dave was different. He was able to hold his own corner. He got on well with people, and he mixed with everyone. It didn't matter to him who you were or what background you had. The other lads from Dublin never mixed and they stuck together in a corner, and they would cry and that sort of thing. We noticed that he mixed well with country people.

'David's other brothers were in the school too. They played football [Gaelic], and they were good. They walked up and down to school together, but they were in with different teachers.

'Where he lived was a wonderful place for a young boy to grow up because they could swim in the canal just nearby. They also had the old mill to play around and then all the private laneways. The canal was only about a hundred yards away. I would have thought David would have had good memories of living there. I always felt it was a children's paradise.'

The sudden influx of people into rural areas stretched the resources of the small communities that found themselves tripled in size overnight. Food was at a premium anyway, and a lot of people just didn't have the money to support themselves. Paddy Egan explained, 'The local priest was in charge of locating people in the houses, so they would have had an input into who went where. The priest was also a civil defence officer as well. LSFs they were called at the time, Local Security Force, and LDF was Local Defence Force. The LSF was made up of people who wouldn't be considered for the army, like the local teacher or the local priest. It was those kinds of people who looked after the families. They even kept a watch out for people who drank. It wasn't acceptable in those days, so one of them would have called round on a visit. That's what the times were like. And we used to call the people "the evacuees". We knew that word even though we were young. But they were part of the community. As Dublin people coming in, the Tynan O'Mahonys mixed a bit *extra* well, at least in comparison to other Dublin people who came in. The others didn't make as many friends. At that time local people took very quick to strangers coming in. At that time rural people were very welcoming. It isn't the same nowadays.

'Mrs Tynan O'Mahony was a very erect woman and good-looking. She carried herself very well. She would walk down the village, and I can remember her with her great red coat. It was a two-mile walk through the countryside lanes from their house to ours. She would come up to our house and stay a while. I remember my mother bringing her in, and they talked for hours. She would make herself a guest of the house – she wouldn't just knock on the door and go – and I remember her taking my youngest brother on her knee in our house. She was very much a part of the community, even though they wouldn't have been around that long. The mother called over to our house to buy butter, milk and eggs, which would have been considered fairly fortunate. For a local family to be able to get a pound of butter would have been an achievement. She was well able to go and knock on doors and get the necessities. The family was well fed.'

It was not the same for the rest of the evacuees and residents at the time. Paddy continued, 'There was terrible poverty around then, but I never remember that family as having been in that poverty trap. For example you definitely wouldn't class them as being poor. They were very comfortable.'

When the family moved back to Dublin, it appears that Dave and his brothers lost contact with everyone in Keenagh. 'David never made any contact with us again, though. He always denied his life here. Keenagh didn't exist as far as he was concerned. He never, ever, spoke of it again, and he never told anyone how he lost the finger. The first I heard of him being famous was around 1963 when he went on the BBC. Straight away he was recognised by local people. I remember a local fellow said to me, "Do you remember David O'Mahony going to school?" And I said to him, "Yes, I do. I was in the one class with him." And he said, "That's the fellow that's Dave Allen on the BBC." That's when I knew it was him and I remembered him.'

Paddy continued, 'At the time you were talking about a very Catholic Ireland and people didn't talk about ... sex,' he said in a low voice, 'and all the other things that go along with it. The likes of my mother would say, "Oh, that dirty bastard." It got a bad reception around here. He wouldn't have been celebrated for some of his work, and I saw some of his stuff and even by today's standards it is fairly strong,' he added, nodding. 'I would say I'm fairly tolerant and I would have learned to live with it.'

But the people of Keenagh were disappointed in him, not just because he didn't ever visit them or mention them again, but as Paddy Egan said, 'People were disappointed that he took the approach that he did and that he was the subject of a debate in the British Parliament. They didn't want him on the BBC at all. The BBC were shocked over it.'

It doesn't sound as if Dave Allen would have been welcome back in Keenagh at all, but Paddy disagreed: 'I think it would have made a difference if he came back. He would have drawn a crowd. We would have been pleased to see him.'

By 1943 it was obvious that Dublin was not going to be targeted by the Luftwaffe again, and the Tynan O'Mahony family returned to Corky and Cherryfield. Neighbours had noticed that Corky's behaviour was even more eccentric after having been on his own for eighteen months. They were used to him never being around when the family had been there. They thought him a workaholic and a bit of a spendthrift, the way he took taxis everywhere. But now there were strange tales of him sitting on an upturned bucket out in the garden of the big house in the pouring rain for hours on end by himself.

The family's trouble didn't just appear to be the emotional state of Corky; their financial state was becoming perilous. There were stories locally that Corky was drinking and gambling heavily and had been ever since the family had left. As their neighbour in Firhouse, Paddy O'Toole, remembers, 'Corky used to send the boys off with a cheque for fourpence or sixpence sometimes to go to the cinema. I don't know if they cashed it, or what would have happened if they did, but they used to get in anyway. They tried to get a bit of a laugh out if it. They'd be slightly embarrassed by it, but they wouldn't mind really. You didn't get embarrassed about much back in those days. It was tough for everyone.'

The Tynan O'Mahony boys returned to their friends and

their old haunts and routines. They spent Saturday afternoons either at the now demolished Corinthian cinema in Dublin, down at the Quays, or at the Classic in Terenure. Dave and Johnny nicknamed the Corinthian 'the Ranch' as they always watched cowboy pictures there. They took the bus into Dublin, and Johnny would entertain the whole bus with jokes and stories. David later told tales about letting other kids in to the cinema who had no money by waiting for the lights to go out and then running down to the exits to open the doors and let everyone in. The three brothers discovered that if they dipped pennies in acid while they were at school, they would shine like shillings. They knew that the lady at the box office at the cinema was so short-sighted that she used to give David and his brothers eight pence in change from their fake 'shillings'. They gave the usherettes a difficult time too – chewing their tickets so that if the usherettes came to check them the boys had to pull the soggy, disgusting mess out of their mouths and, horrified, the usherettes would walk away. The three boys were always up to something and had quite a reputation in their neighbourhood.

Dave would tell of the times when his father would sit all the kids down and tell them stories. All the children would listen, entranced. Corky would gather the three boys around him, and they made a circle of 'wagons' out of the chairs and the sofa and lit the fire. Then his father would turn out the lights, and the boys would sit and listen, just like Dave did as a younger child in the pub. He said that the stories had not necessarily been funny or scary, just stories. He said that he had done this when his children were small too, just telling them anything that came into his head.

His father's storytelling was the inspiration that would stay with the youngest Tynan O'Mahony until he became Dave Allen and would create his own form of storytelling that sadly his father would never see.

The neighbours and school friends were becoming increasingly aware that times were tough for the family. The family had a maid for domestic duties while both parents worked who everyone remembers as being very nice, but she left. Everyone was aware that keeping the three boys at good schools would be a drain on the family's diminishing resources.

In 1945 Dave Allen went to St Mary's in Rathmines. John Kennedy, another neighbour used to walk to school with him. 'I walked Dave to school most days. He was jovial even for a young lad, but I got the impression he didn't have that many friends in that school.

'He was always building tree houses, even in school. Dave used to pull mine down. I was the younger, so he'd always play pranks on me. There was one time he'd finished making his tent and he came into ours and was sharing around a bottle of Taylor Keith red lemonade. I put my mouth to it. It was awful. He had filled it with urine. That taste never leaves me. It still sticks in me craw [sic].'

Although Dave would say that he wasn't religious, the three boys – Peter, John and David – were brought up as Roman Catholics, while his mother, Jean, was a converted Anglican and his father, Corky, was an agnostic. The fact that Dave's father was even associated with a Roman

Catholic family but worked at a protestant newspaper, the *Irish Times*, was highly unusual. It wasn't until the eighties that you could buy a copy of the paper without 'crossing the lines' to find a Protestant newspaper shop that would stock it.

'Of course at this time the second most important thing in Ireland after your name was whether you were Protestant or Roman Catholic. At job interviews you were asked your name and then immediately, "Catholic or Protestant?" It was more important than your experience or qualifications. The school that you went to, Catholic or Protestant, would mark you for life,' said Patricia Smyllie.

Patricia remembers her first encounter with Dave Allen: 'I first met Dave in 1943. He was just seven years old and was upside down in a basket at the time. I had been evacuated from London to live with relatives in Dublin. It wasn't a conventional meeting at all. Dave's father worked for my uncle, Robert Maire Smyllie, who was the editor of the *Irish Times*. Smyllie was a huge personality. He always rode a bicycle to work, regardless of his sobriety, wearing pyjamas, a fisherman's sweater and to complete the ensemble he wore a green sombrero. At twenty-two stone he cut quite a vision. Imagine seeing that character riding the streets of Dublin each day.

'Smyllie used to stand in the middle of the office and sing parts of his leading articles in operatic recitative to the assembled journalists. He had shaped the nail on his little finger into a pen nib, just like Keats. He was not a man to be tampered with.

'My uncle's office was sacrosanct, small, with high

wooden walls and was not the sort of place you would expect to see a seven-year-old boy being chased around. But this almost hallowed place was where I saw little Dave's legs kicking around in this huge fisherman's basket that Smyllie filled with used copy paper.

'Smyllie just screamed from the office, "Pussy!" which was Dave's father's nickname at the paper, and asked him to explain who this boy was, and he replied, "It is my youngest, sir." The next thing I remember is Dave's father holding him [Dave] in one hand by the ankles while deftly hitting him over his bottom with a large metal ruler. The little boy of seven obviously thought the whole incident a huge joke and couldn't stop laughing while his father chased him around Smyllie's holiest of holies. "Hitting Davie has no effect on him. None the slightest," explained "Pussy".' She continued, 'Dave's father, Cullen O'Mahony, was an extremely funny man, even funnier when he had had a few drinks. I think that he always regretted that he had stuck to journalism, as he rather fancied himself treading the boards as an actor. He had the nickname "Pussy" at work because he was a great cat lover. It sounds quite effeminate to us now, but it was purely to do with his love of cats. Every morning the first thing he did was to feed the cats when he arrived at the office, even if he was still quite wobbly and hung-over. The cats were crucial to the newspaper. Their job was to keep down the rats and the mice at the newspaper's warehouses near O'Connor Bridge in Dublin. These warehouses were where the enormous rolls of newsprint were stored. As this was during the war, not only did my uncle, the editor of the paper, have to get permission from the IRA when they needed to order newsprint, it then also had to make the precarious crossing across the Atlantic from Canada dodging all the U-boats. It was very precious stuff. The cats were the protectors of the newsprint.'

On 19 April 1948 the family's future changed overnight. Pussy, or Corky, like most of the male side of the family, died at an early age. He was barely fifty. Dave, as the youngest son, had lost the man who adored him, who gave him cuddles and was the inspiration for his storytelling. The family was devastated, not only emotionally but, as they were to discover, financially as well.

'Everyone thought the family was relatively prosperous, but that changed when his father suddenly died.' Cahill O'Shannon, whose father was also a columnist at the *Irish Times*, continued, 'It was rather terrible because when Pussy suddenly died quite young, there was no money in the bank. Instead there were huge debts from his drinking. We were all really surprised that the family had been left in such a destitute state,' Cahill explained.

Everyone knew that something had to be done to help this family. Pussy had been popular at the newspaper, and everyone liked the family. The journalists at the *Irish Times* took action. Cahill continued, 'The family were so impover-ished that my father, along with Smyllie, the editor, Bruce Williamson, the leader writer, and Myles na Gopaleen [Flann O'Brien] ordered everyone at the newspaper to pay half a crown, two shillings and sixpence out of their weekly wages into a special fund to keep the family going.

'Pussy had always drunk heavily and was into gambling, which was a disaster for the family. Half a crown may not seem a lot of money nowadays, but it was nearly twenty-five per cent of some of the journalists' weekly wage.'

With an income from only the goodwill of the journalists to survive on, the family were heading for even tougher times. There was not a lot of money for a mother and three boys to live on.

The changes that happened to the close-knit Tynan O'Mahony family were almost instant, and as the youngest child, the death of his beloved father hit the twelve-year-old Dave very hard. Standing at his father's graveside in Tallaght, the future seemed bleak to the boy who would completely change the face of comedy.

One schoolmate remembers, 'Looking back, I'd say Dave had some fairly tough times in school. We all had tough times back then, I suppose, but it was apparent sometimes from his attire, although he'd never say anything. You definitely would have spotted the guy as going through financial difficulties. There were a couple of times when you noticed he wasn't as well prepared as he should have been.'

The twelve-year-old Dave Allen suddenly found himself in a very different environment at Terenure College, away from his friends and his brothers, who had left school and were starting out to find work to support the family. Even though he had changed schools, his day-to-day routine didn't alter much. He played football, although the general consensus is badly; he had never been that interested academically, and the art classes did not suit his style. He enjoyed drawing cartoons and did not like being told what to draw. The priests took the majority of the classes and do not appear to have been overly strict. None of his school friends had any complaints about how they were treated. (Interestingly he was not a boarder at any of the schools he attended, so the later nightmare visions of priests swooping around dormitories were simply very clever tales, possibly created from stories that others had told him.) He just could not wait to get out of school and start earning. This impatience was a big problem for him and his teachers and family.

The friendly, quiet, intelligent boy underwent a radical transformation following the death of his father. There was no one there to tell him stories or for him to watch in the pub, nor spank him. The sudden lack of income affected the whole family and Dave had to change schools. While Dave Tynan O'Mahony was generally acknowledged to have been a prankster and always looking for mischief, he discovered now that he could fight.

'School in Ireland was a rough training ground in the 'forties,' Pat Smyllie explained. 'If you take something as normal as a school sports day or a hockey match, there would be two sets of ambulances on the sidelines: one for Catholics and one for Protestants. I had been moved out to Dublin at the start of the war from London. At my school we were told that if we were losing to the "other" side, then we should just hit the other girls. Broken noses and jaws were commonplace. We were judged solely on injuries doled out. If we had any injuries ourselves, then we would be perceived to have lost and out would come the strap and we would be beaten for failing. When I returned to England, I was banned from playing hockey at Cheltenham Ladies' College as I played too rough.'

Dave Allen developed his own way of surviving on this 'battlefield'. Michael McKenna was a friend of Dave's and a classmate at Terenure College from 1947 until 1949. 'He was a terrible nice guy, a real good guy, but, my God, he was as hard as nails. We called him "Tarzan". In spite of his fairly genteel and intellectual surroundings at home, Dave had developed the instincts of a hard man.'

Dave became a forthright and fearless teenager. Having little time for academic or sporting achievement, he regularly faced down bullies and was renowned, or perhaps notorious, for his jab. They say he became the 'black sheep' of the family, perhaps because of the long history of literary achievement set in train by Katharine Tynan. McKenna continued, 'Certainly as he neared his time in Terenure, Dave had thrown to the wind any notions of academia.

'He'd always be up to sheer devilment. We're talking absolute messing. We were always out robbing orchards and climbing trees. He was a tough guy. He would take a shortcut and beat up all the bullies blocking his way! But he'd never be unfair. He could've been a great bully himself, but he just wasn't like that. There *was* a bully in our class. He tried to pick a fight with me, but "Tarzan" took care of him. It was pure fists – there was nothing else in them days – but he gave him a right seeing-to. A full grown man would never have gone near him, and he wasn't especially big either. He would have been average height.

'Out of all the people in our class, Dave never tried to stand out. Dave was very fair-minded. He only used his physical capabilities as a defence mechanism, but he wasn't cowed by any discipline. He was a real survivor.' Michael McKenna continued, 'When I think back, Dave was the nearest thing you'd have to a great warrior – he's the kind of person who would have been the first to go into battle. He had all the courage in the world, and nobody would ever beat him.'

Devastated by the loss of his father and frustrated at not being able to go out to work to help the family, he appeared to have responsibilities beyond his years. Dave Tynan O'Mahony became a problem at school.

Despite showing much understanding and patience after the death of his father, and following meetings, warnings and discussions with his mother, the priests at the school finally had enough of the tough, uncontrollable teenage warrior, and in 1949, a year after his father had died, Dave was expelled from Terenure College. Or, as one neighbour politely put it, 'The priests asked the family to take him out.' Another neighbour remembers, 'I don't know what happened to him, but you can be sure it was some kind of mischief.' After Terenure it's believed Dave was sent on to the Catholic University School on Leeson Street.

Friends say that Peter was the most academic of the boys and that in later years Dave resented the fact that his eldest brother saw better times and had more opportunities. They felt that Dave was in denial about the hardships and realities of the life he faced as a child, one of the reasons why he remained so reluctant to elaborate on his youth.

'I honestly felt he was never happy in school. He wasn't turned on by it, even though he had the brains and intellectual basis in the family. Although he was highly intelligent, he always struck me as a guy in a hurry to go somewhere and school held him back,' said Paddy O'Toole. 'We weren't at all surprised when he became famous, but it was his style that surprised me. As a practising Catholic, I didn't like it. Whenever he came home, though, for the rugby, he would always drop into Delaney's.'

In later years Dave would explain that when the clergy, 'the Gestapo in drag', weren't taunting him for his luck, or lack of it, they were forcing him to believe in religious doctrine that he neither understood nor cared to. Dave said that he was 'educated with the Holy Ghost Fathers, the Carmelite Fathers and touched by the Dominicans and the Loreto Nuns plus the odd skirmish with the Christian Brothers'. He said, 'They would literally beat the fear of God into you. We were told to watch out for the Devil each night, that if we had an erection, then that was the Devil coming to get us. Imagine saying that to a young boy. It was terrifying.'

It was not easy for the young Dave Tynan O'Mahony, and all the while he was being watched over by 'God's storm troopers'. Meanwhile his brother, John, had started work at Independent Newspapers, and Peter was a junior reporter and photographer at the *Drogheda Times*, doing what Dave dreamed of doing – escaping and earning money. He knew that he had to help his mother too.

'I believe that Dave was incredibly traumatised by the loss of his father. Then the change of lifestyle made him ashamed. He was astonished and hurt by the way his mother's relations viewed his family's financial mess. You know, he refused to speak about any of this, even years later. He built up this defensive wall even around all of us who had known him for so long,' said Patricia Smyllie. The young Dave Allen was learning to lock away his memories, to compartmentalise them.

One story that appeared in the act was about his mother telling him as a small child to walk on the outside to protect 'his mummy'. During the act he tells how his mother went on to explain that it was to 'keep his sword arm free'. The child by now in the routine is crying; he claims that he 'doesn't have a sword', so she goes on to say that he is being stupid and it is in case a double-decker bus runs into them. The bus will hit the child first, and 'mummy will be safe'. The child then gets a perfunctory 'thwack' with the microphone for crying in terror at the prospect of being run over by a bus.

Dave went on to speak about a child's fear at night, when his mother would tell him to 'watch out for the Sandman', or 'the night goblins', and how could anyone expect a child ever get to sleep with the prospect of a man visiting each child's room to sprinkle sand in their eyes or of bogeymen hiding under the bed? And of course there were the tales of the priests roaming the dormitories at night, with small faces hiding under the sheets in terror. A lot of his routines were based on the terror of a child, frightened by the Church, their parent's exasperation, or by life.

There are a lot of stories about the loss of Dave's finger, most of them invented by Dave himself. They all seem to come from his childhood. He used to joke that he lost it when his father threatened to cut off his finger if Dave did not stop picking his nose. Dave ignored the warning, so his father put his finger on a stump and raised his axe. A game of chicken ensued, and the top of the forefinger on his left hand was severed.

On hearing this, Cahill O'Shannon laughed, 'No, that was just a story. His father was dead long before Dave lost the top of his finger. He lost it in his own accident; I don't know how. But as for his father chopping it off, he would have been too drunk to chop any wood, and Pussy certainly wasn't the type to play around like that. If he had done anything like that, we would have all heard of it. Maybe you will discover how it happened yourself.'

Finally Dave was able to leave school, but without completing his Leaving Certificate. He managed to get a job at Independent Newspapers working with his brother, Johnny, in one of the back offices. 'You were expected to get a good, safe job, and following in the footsteps of your father was a safe option,' said Patricia Smyllie. 'The women all liked the good-looking O'Mahony brothers, although it was Johnny who had the jokes and stories and was the centre of attention.'

When John left the newspaper to go to England, Dave moved over to the *Drogheda Argus* to work with his other brother, Peter. It was at the *Argus* that there are the most vivid memories of him. An obituary printed by the paper (which subsequently closed its Drogheda office and is now solely based in Dundalk) remembers Dave as having had a crush on an older girl called Nora, but there are no further details about her.

But the work at the newspaper that he was doing didn't appeal to him. Indeed some believe that he did little in the way of journalism there and was everything from teaboy to copyboy. After some time Dave followed his brother, John, over to England. Their mother followed in 1955. With two jobs in just one year, the restless Dave Allen tried his luck in London at many of the newspapers. He had plenty of charm, but with no qualifications he had no luck.

Every spring, all the newspapers in England ran an advertisement for people to become Butlins 'Redcoats' for the forthcoming season. With a guaranteed roof over your head, four square meals and a licence to entertain for twelve hours a day, it didn't take Johnny O'Mahony long to realise that this is what he wanted to do. He also discovered that he was extremely good at it, some say even funnier than Dave.

Johnny joined Butlins holiday camp as a Redcoat at Filey, and he was in his element. He phoned his brother and persuaded Dave to leave St Albans, where he was living with his mother, because it would 'be fun'.

Dave Tynan O'Mahony didn't have to wait long before he could try out the storytelling skills that he had learned from his father. He was just nineteen in 1955 when serendipity intervened and showed him the way to a career that would endure for forty years.

CHAPTER TWO

─────────

BUTLINS-BY-THE-SEA

'I saw the very first time that Dave sat on a stool and told stories. We were both working as Redcoats at Butlins. This would be the winter of 1956,' remembers ex-Butlins Redcoat Lynda Noon. 'We had been out for a ramble. This meant that the Redcoats, Dave and I in this instance, took out a load of campers for a walk all around Saltdean, Rottingdean, all over the cliffs and back to camp. It had started to rain really heavily, and Dave and I led the campers back to the Ocean Hotel in Brighton and into the ballroom before everyone got soaked. The ballroom was laid out with seats in a semi-circle, and we had about four hundred people with us, so it was packed.

'Dave looked at me and said, "This is hopeless. What are we going to do?" Then he picked up a bar stool and took it into the middle of the ballroom and told me that I didn't have to stay, but I did; I was fascinated. Dave O'Mahony just sat there and, unrehearsed and unplanned, he told stories and jokes for about an hour. Everyone listened, transfixed. This was totally different to what we used to do as Redcoats. It was a huge success.'

It would be some years before the young Dave Allen would get the opportunity to use his storytelling skills in his act again.

In 1955, following their short careers in journalism, the O'Mahony brothers had found a way to earn a living and gain valuable experience in the entertainment industry by working at Butlins. For at least five months of the year they had guaranteed free board and lodging and they were even given clothes to wear.

With its fairly strict regime of schedules and uniform, but surrounded by people wanting to be entertained, this was a discipline that appealed to the brothers. They both knew that this would provide some much-needed work experience, whether it was in entertainment or anything else. Dave would also be miles away from his childhood experiences of schools and of the Church, where he described the confessional as talking to 'God's middle-man, a ninety-five-year-old bigot'. During the three years that Dave worked as a Redcoat he moved from Skegness, to Filey, Margate, and then Brighton for the winter seasons. His brother, Johnny, would stay on as a Redcoat until 1966.

'Every year, Butlins advertised in all the local papers that they were looking for people to work as Redcoats. They used to interview thousands and whittle them down to the possibles. We asked them if they had stage ambitions and if they said yes, then we told them they were a Redcoat first and an entertainer second,' said Roger

Billington, the archivist at Butlins Bognor Regis.

Dave O'Mahony (he had dropped the 'Tynan'), like all the hopefuls, was told at his interview, 'A Redcoat is also an individual, a character, a personality girl [or boy], a sporting type, a sing-song leader, a bingo caller, a children's uncle, a swimmer, a dancer, but – above all – a mixer, a mingler. A Redcoat works a hard and tiring day – whose ready smile is just as genuine last thing at night as it was at breakfast time.' For some of the Redcoats this meant working nearly twenty hours a day.

The first Butlins camp opened at Skegness in 1936 at a then huge cost of £50,000. Families could stay there for 'two pounds, five shillings a week and four good meals a day'. During the war signs went up at all the camps: 'Will re-open once we have finished with Hitler.' The War Department realised early on in the war that Butlins was the only organisation in the UK that had the experience of mass catering. The Royal Marines trained in the tropical swimming pools, paraded in the ballrooms, and dentists held their surgeries under signs that read 'Madame Rosy, Clairvoyant'. One of the camps was converted into an internment camp for German nationals who had found themselves in England at the start of the war. After the war the camp at Filey was opened. It could accommodate, and feed of course, 9,000 campers.

In post-war austerity England Butlins had a reputation for value-for-money family holidays. The camps were even considered to be extremely sophisticated places; everyone from royalty to the clergy had visited Butlins. In the brochures it claimed that just arriving at Butlins felt as though you were in a movie with fountains playing at the front of each camp. By 1986 it was estimated that ten million adults had visited Butlins in England.

Always located along the coast, the camps specialised in entertainment for the whole family, with talent contests, bingo, dances and funfair-type rides. Holidaymakers stayed in basic but cheerfully presented chalets. They became used to being woken up over the tannoy each morning with 'Good morning, campers' and the now world-famous 'Hi-de-hi' call. Crucially for teenagers and singles, the camps provided great opportunities to escape from the watchful eyes of parents. 'We all had a great time, including the Redcoats,' said Roger Billington.

The camps were to prove to be a valuable training ground for anyone with a hint of talent from comics to singers. Many of the household names that hit the television screens in the sixties and seventies had started out at Butlins, including Roy Hudd, Freddie Davis, Jimmy Tarbuck, Des O'Connor and, of course, Dave Allen. Roger Billington said, 'Roy Hudd told them at his interview that he played the piano. One day they needed a piano moving and the entertainment manager remembered that Roy had mentioned the word piano. That was the nearest he got to playing one – moving it!'

Butlins appeared to suit Dave, with the smart uniform of red blazer, white shirt and white trousers for the men. He was learning new skills every day. Johnny and he were in their element. There was a great camaraderie and team spirit. 'You could hide behind the uniform and lots of people did. You wouldn't recognise some of them out of season,' said Rocky Mason, a long-time friend of Dave's and a fellow Redcoat.

Roger Billington continued, 'When you put on your red blazer and white trousers, apart from being very conspicuous, it made you bigger somehow, and I used to feel marvellous. It was a very good life. In the sixties we were paid well: nine pounds a week. We got free board and all our food and clothes to wear. We were carefully watched so that we didn't make any rude remarks even jokingly about the food. On top of that we all got coffee-bar vouchers. As we were meant to sit with the campers, or guests, even when we were not working, we had about seven shillings' worth of vouchers each week so we could buy coffees or whatever while we were socialising. We used to save them up sometimes and have a big party in one of the chalets. We had a very good life during the season, and you felt completely lost when the season ended. You had to go and find whatever work you could until the next season started again.'

Dave O'Mahony did everything from bingo calling to a stage routine. 'He wasn't so keen on the sports stuff, though,' remembers Rocky Mason. 'He used to do this Jerry Lewis impersonation later at Filey. He was really so talented, and everyone liked both of the O'Mahony brothers. Johnny was the camp "tramp", which meant he didn't shave for a week, went around in huge trousers with string round them. Every camp had a "tramp". On Friday Johnny changed into his blazer and trousers, had a shave for the first time in a week, and when he went on stage all the girls used to scream, because he was so good-looking.

'Dave would never have offered to be the "tramp". He

even chatted up the wardrobe mistress to alter his blazer and taper his white trousers. He was always immaculately dressed.

'Dave and Johnny worked hard to build their acts. Dave was really into the American comics, which was why he did the whole Jerry Lewis thing with the accent, and he quiffed his hair to look just like Lewis,' remembers Rocky.

It was at Butlins that Dave started to enjoy scaring his audiences. He was trying out the ghost stories and tales that his father had told Johnny, Peter and himself. Rocky Mason remembers, 'Oh, there was a great routine that he would do; he loved scaring people. Dave would sit on a dark stage with a green spotlight on his face. The whole place was silent. He started in a whisper, and there was not a sound as they listened to this long, rambling tale, and he asked them whether they believed in ghosts and spirits. What the audience didn't know was that he had a starting pistol hidden behind the chair and that there were Redcoats standing at the back of the hall ready to scare everyone.

'He went on about driving over the moors. The car broke down, and he found an empty house. As he told them about opening the door to the house, he would fire the starting pistol and the front five rows would leap out of their seats. He would continue telling the story, up the stairs, and trying each locked door, then finally he found a door that opened. It led into a room full of spiders dangling down in his face. Right at that moment all the Redcoats would throw handfuls of rice over the audience and they screamed their heads off as they thought it was the spiders. It was great stuff. Because I said to Dave how much I enjoyed the ghost routine, he said to me, "You have it." He was incredibly generous,' says Rocky Mason.

'Johnny and Dave were very creative,' Rocky continues. 'One moment they were quietly spoken, intellectual Irishmen, the next they were clowns. They came up with a gag for firing a man out of a cannon. Of course it was a fake, with a "double" standing over by the net but hidden out of sight, ready to look as if he had been fired from it. Johnny used to add more and more explosive until people refused to get in it. It was a great success, but they were so generous they always credited me with the "Cannon of Death". You see, they were the ideas men, but I was the one who welded these two dustbins together as I thought it was such a great gag. Johnny and Dave would never have organised it. They just came up with the most amazing routines and ideas.'

As a family-orientated business, Butlins had special services for young children and babies that allowed parents to go and watch a show knowing that one of the chalet patrols would hear if there was any crying from any of the chalets. Roger Billington remembers, 'Dave suffered from the "baby crying" sign – well, everyone did. It always went off when he was at a tag-line to a great story or joke. There were electric signs at the side of the stage. If the chalet patrol that walked around the site constantly in the evening had heard a child crying, then the sign would suddenly start flashing, "Baby crying, blue block Z 23", and it always went off at a crucial moment.

'There would be an enormous upheaval in the audience as the worried parents would get up to go and deal with the crying baby, and Dave, like all the performers, would be left standing there wondering whether to abandon the story or repeat the lead-in to the tag.'

Butlins had a reputation for good, clean entertainment, and even the young Dave Allen would have to fit in with this regime. Roger explains about Sir Billy Butlin and his attitude to jokes about sex and the Church, 'There was a sign in the wings of each theatre at the camps. It had a large header saying, "NO BLUE MATERIAL". It went on to say, "May we remind all artists that Butlins caters for family audiences, and despite the permissive world outside, we intend to maintain our standards. Do not use offensive or explicit material as children don't understand it and parents don't like it." We all had to obey that sign. For one thing, you never knew when Sir Billy Butlin was going to do a surprise visit.

'One Sunday afternoon there was a band call to rehearse all the acts for that evening. Each camp had a review company, and that night a rather good vocalist had come over from Minehead for a rehearsal. Alf Reid was the musical director. He couldn't understand why this girl came on to the stage crying her eyes out. He told her that nothing could be that bad and to stop crying. She said that she was devastated as she had bought a blue dress to wear for that night, but the sign said, "NO BLUE MATERIAL", so she couldn't wear it. You couldn't make it up, could you? They were more innocent times back then.'

After a very successful first season at Filey, in the winter of 1955/56 Dave was one of the few Redcoats chosen to work the winter season. He moved to the Ocean Hotel in Brighton. He had very good company at High Lodge, the

Redcoats' home in Saltdean; he was sharing with a young comic from Liverpool, Jimmy Tarbuck, who later became godfather to Dave's son, Edward.

Lynda Noon (wife of organist Jimmy Noon) worked with Dave Allen at the hotel in Brighton. She said, 'You had to be very good to be offered a winter season at Butlins. Everyone wanted to stay on, but they had to approach you. You couldn't apply. Dave and I worked at Brighton all through that winter. Johnny and Dave O'Mahony were both highly talented. Dave and Johnny both worked at Margate too. The life suited them.'

Dave O'Mahony hadn't yet started to exclude his childhood and he was happy to tell everyone about their lives back in Dublin. After Butlins, though, his childhood was never talked about again and his time at Butlins became a shortened version.

Dee Piggott who also worked with Dave at Brighton said, 'We would all meet up in one of the chalets after work. When we were sitting around after a really long day, Dave would sit and tell us stories and tell us about his childhood. Most of the Redcoats were smokers and drinkers, and we had some good times sitting listening to Dave.

'He reckoned that he had been to eight schools in twelve years and told us with a completely straight face that his father had chopped his finger off as a punishment for picking his nose. I think we believed him too. But there were things, though, that you could tell were true. He told us about his childhood in Firhouse and how he and his brothers played tricks on courting couples. They used to spy them in the grass and surreptitiously creep up on them. On a given signal, the three of them would lob cow pats at the unsuspecting couples. The poor things. He thought this was hysterical. His parents must have been exasperated with the three boys. He also told us in great complicated detail about how he had bitten off the end of his tongue when he was three or four and how it had been sewn back on. We all sat and listened to these tales.

'There was a whole gang of us who were friends at the time: Kay Bassano, Molly Richardson, Lynda and I. Dave used to tell us all about how he wanted to travel the world. We just listened to these great plans, never thinking that it would all come true for him.'

At this point, though, although practising his tale-telling with the Redcoats, there are no memories of the drawing or painting that he had started as a child and that would sustain him on tour much later.

Dee continued about working with Dave in Brighton, 'Dave was always flirting with all of us. He was a good-looking young guy of nineteen or so, and you couldn't tell whether he was serious or not. I was married at the time to Wally, another Redcoat, but that didn't seem to matter. I always thought that he would never have gone out with someone taller than him at that stage. It probably wouldn't have mattered to him later.'

Lynda Noon continued, 'Dave and Johnny were completely different. Some days you could go up to Johnny and he would seem miles away, not with any of us at all, and the next day he would be back to normal and the life and soul of the party. I got the feeing that Johnny followed Dave around everywhere, just tagged along.'

Lynda Noon had realised that Johnny was not only a completely different character to Dave, but that he also needed a friend to watch over him. 'In Margate, this would be in '56, Johnny took out all the kids and went into a cafe to buy thirty-five ice creams. He collected all the ice creams and sat the kids down in the cafe. You can see how they must have taken over the cafe with all those kids.

'Of course the cafe owner came over and told him to clear off. Johnny led all the kids outside and proceeded to teach them how to shop-lift. You can imagine the tales that got back to the parents and everyone about this little escapade. He was an outrageous character really. I remember one day for some reason he had hundreds of cigarettes and he just sat in the bar and handed them out free to everyone. He was hopeless with money. I used to look after it for him and hand it out to him when he needed it. He was such a talented guy, and I knew he needed help.

'His was a tale of missed opportunities. I know that lots of meetings were arranged with talent scouts and agents, just like Dave had, but Johnny would never show up. He was considered to be unreliable but hugely talented. It was such a waste and a great shame.'

Laurie Boynton, a Redcoat from Filey, continued, 'Johnny was a terrible gambler. He really would bet on two flies crawling up a wall. But his health was dreadful. He had bad stomach ulcers and ignored them. One winter he had to stay with a friend of mine rather than work the winter in Brighton. He would never go to hospital. He even had to swap from Guinness to milk.

'Strangely, Johnny was very envious of me and the rest of

us who had done National Service. I suppose because Dave and he were from Ireland they didn't have to do it. It really rankled him that he had missed out.

'In 1967 Johnny ended up working for Johnny Romaine, emptying slot machines for him. Then of course later on he went to work at several theatres in London. He was a very good stage hand.'

Lynda Noon said, 'The last time I saw Dave was at the funeral of Mike Grogan. He had been a Redcoat too and was Russ Conway's right-hand man. We used to get messages from Dave down the years from various people saying that he sent his love. It was a thrill watching Dave, Jimmy Tarbuck and all of them become famous.'

After Brighton, for the summer of 1957, Dave moved to Skegness, leaving Johnny in Filey on his own. 'I was the only one who had a car so I used to run Johnny down to Skegness to see Dave in the show,' said Rocky Mason, 'and Dave used to come and see Johnny at the Empire Theatre in Filey. He did a late-night show called *O'Mahony's Madness* on a Tuesday night, and I did one on a Thursday called *Rendezvous with Rocky*. Dave would always sit and make notes and then give you his ideas on how to improve your act. Johnny was always considered to be funnier than Dave. The campers used to complain that Dave spoke too fast and that it was difficult to understand him.'

But the problem for Johnny O'Mahony was that he didn't really have an act and he had a love of drinking. With all his time spent gambling, drinking and doing his Redcoat duties, the two brothers would start to move apart professionally.

With the majority of Redcoats harbouring 'show-business'

dreams, it must have been difficult to give everyone the opportunity to shine. 'All the Redcoats did sketches, whether they were showbiz inclined or not. It didn't take long to spot that someone had talent. You could tell Dave was good. He used to watch everyone and learn from them; he was continually revising what he did,' remembers Dizzie Leslie, who ran the review company at Skegness.

'We created an act called "Threesomes". Dave, Lou Grant and Dennis Hayward went on and did an act as triplets. There was a movie at the time called *Triplets* and we based it on that. Apart from Dave in Skegness, we had Freddie Davis as well, so there was a lot of talent about.

'But everyone loved Dave O'Mahony. I remember him riding through the camp on Saucy the elephant from one end of the camp to the other. There were always hoards of people following him. It looked like a huge parade and he loved it. At the "Au Revoir" show for the campers on their last night, which was always a Friday, Dave O'Mahony got such a cheer when he came on stage. All the campers liked him and knew that he worked eighteen hours a day. But you know, it was very hard work, and I am not sure he liked it that much as we really weren't paid very much. The seasons were long from May to September, and then you had to find other work. It was a culture shock to a lot of people finding themselves back in the outside world.

'Some of us went to see him at his first booking outside Butlins at the ex-servicemen's club [The London Casino, now the Prince Edward Theatre]. You didn't get paid for appearing there. He was very raw. We were sorry that he didn't keep in touch.'

For all the hard work and the eighteen-hour-long days, Dave Allen stayed at Butlins for nearly four years of winter and summer seasons, finding his feet in the profession that he would later say 'I fell into'. While Dave was fond of his brother and watched out for him all his life, he was probably aware that professionally their lives would have to part. With his love of drinking and gambling, Johnny was not going to be the perfect touring partner for Dave. There were stories about Johnny rigging the competitions, having run-ins and arguments with the management, and then there were the many missed appointments and opportunities. The two brothers parted company as performers, but Dave was always to keep in touch with his brother and help him through the years.

In Filey Dave had met another talented comic, Al Page. Dave teamed up with Al and decided to go out on the road as a double act. They left Butlins and started touring the club circuit. They based their act on Jerry Lewis and Dean Martin. Red Brigden, a former Redcoat at Filey, met up with them in Sheffield: 'I was performing in panto. I used to be a singer, and one night Dave and Al came to the Lyceum Theatre in Sheffield to see me. They invited me to join them on a gig at the Shoulder of Mutton in Altringham, just outside Sheffield. I went on and performed the opening number, then Dave and Al came on and did their routine. It was very "of the moment". Dave was the straight guy, and Al did the Jerry Lewis act. They did gags, silly stuff really, then ended with a song. I don't think Dave was that keen on the singing part of it, though. He did a very American-style act, very relaxed. He had come on a long way since Butlins. They split up amicably after a while, and Dave went out on his own.'

Meanwhile Johnny was experiencing very mixed fortunes at Butlins. Rocky Mason said, 'There was a mix-up about some Cup Final tickets for Wembley that Johnny had been given by one of the guests. He wasn't interested in going and had passed them on to someone else. Of course the donor of the tickets was surprised to see someone other than Johnny sitting next to him at Wembley. He hadn't sold them or anything; he just didn't want to go. Well, the manager asked Johnny to leave. I think it was a shame, but he eventually came over to me at Bognor Regis.

'Jean O'Mahony, their mother, was always worried about Johnny and his drinking even then,' continues Rocky. 'Now we all drank and smoked, but Johnny really did like his drink. She used to ring me at Bognor and ask me if he was all right. I used to reassure her that he was eating well and that he wasn't drinking too much. She was very concerned about him.

'Johnny did have the opportunity, though, to hit the big time,' said Rocky Mason. 'Dandy Page offered him a gig in Hull, but it didn't go well. There was a rumour that he had been having an affair with a dancer in the company some time before. He went on to do his routine and saw this same girl sitting in the front row. He fired off his opening lines and gags like bullets, said, "Thank you very much," and left the stage. He blew it. He couldn't do his act in front of that girl.

'You know, Johnny was incredibly proud of Dave and his success. There was always a sadness about him, but it wasn't to do with Dave's success at all.'

Dave continued touring clubs, appearing in pantomime and doing shows. He found the life very tough, and he was earning very little. He came up with a plan to keep him at the top of his agent's list.

The story of Dave changing his name has become part of show-business folklore. He had dropped the 'Tynan' by the time he had started at Butlins. Then he discovered that no one could pronounce 'O'Mahony'. When he realised that his agent didn't have any acts with a surname beginning with 'A', he changed his name to Dave Allen, in order to keep his name in the forefront of his agent's mind. It worked and he started to get bigger 'gigs', including Manchester Variety Club.

But touring the clubs, pubs and smaller venues of England in the late fifties was hard work. The audiences were there to drink and be entertained. If you weren't any good, they would let you know immediately by throwing things at you or ignoring you. If you were way down the bill and the first acts were dreadful, then your task in a cigarette-smoke-filled, noisy, hostile room became twice as hard.

At the time Dave Allen was starting out from the safety of Butlins, there had been huge changes to the entertainment industry in England. By the sixties many theatres had closed as the variety circuit had died down. Television was 'blamed' for the change of a theatrical tradition which had started in the early 1900s.

Historian and comic Dr Oliver Double explains, 'The comedians who populated the variety circuits hit the audience with an all-singing, all-dancing style a million miles away from the just-stand-there-behind-a-mike-and-tell-gags approach that we are used to now. Stand-up grew out of singing and music remained a big part of it for decades.'

There was a big difference between the club audience and someone who went to a variety theatre. Oliver Double continued, 'The variety-theatre audience was there to be entertained. They had the opportunity to see thirty acts each performance and watched the indicator board light up at the side of the stage to see when their favourite was coming on.'

The audience could come and go as they pleased. When theatres put on 'culture', opera or ballet at the top of a variety show, then the audience would be packed with people who only turned up to see that. The theatre would be half empty for the rest of the show.

The acts or turns were kept to a rigid schedule, and their billing was crucial (where they appeared on the poster or bill advertising the show). They were allotted a specific amount of time and that was it. If you were the top of the bill, you may be allowed twenty minutes. The usual was just seven or eight minutes. One performer, Joe King, used to time his act by lighting a cigarette as soon as he got on stage: he started his closing song when it burned out. You ran the risk of never being booked again if you over-ran.

The variety-style programme was very much still in vogue, even though television was bringing so many new acts and styles to millions of people. By the late fifties there was a huge diversity of talent offered to people, from comics to 'crooners', stars and dancers.

'One thing that hadn't changed was the content of the comedian's acts. They followed a set tradition of mother-in-law jokes, jokes about any race other than the English, the wife jokes – "She can't cook, she's so ugly, she never stops talking, she's so fat" – anything to do with lavatories and sex. Audiences also liked the ambiguous and the barely disguised sexual innuendo, which was what Larry Grayson and Frankie Howerd did so well. It was predictable and familiar to the audiences. They waited for the catchphrases and reassuring music that accompanied their favourite acts,' Oliver Double.

On the club circuit the comic could be following several others who had just 'died on their feet' or were heckled from the moment they started. The genre was ready for a shake-up, for new, 'alternative' comics.

In 1959 the twenty-three-year-old Dave Allen appeared on a TV talent show in the UK called *New Faces* on ATV, later moving to the BBC. It was his first television appearance. Television was still in its infancy in England, just six years after the very first network television broadcast (for the Coronation) and not many households even had a set.

On *New Faces* a panel of judges was used to 'make scathing' comments on the artist, and then, if they were one of the lucky ones, they were invited back to appear in the final. Dave Allen was given three minutes, told to 'relax, take your time and above all, be "yourself". Dave said that it was the longest, most terrifying three minutes of his life. (Footage of Dave's appearance, along with his result and who won the competition have been lost.)

In 1960 the twenty-four-year-old Dave Allen performed in shows all across the country, including the Birmingham Hippodrome, Salisbury Gaumont and Colston Hall, Bristol.

In the summer Dave joined Hedley Claxton's company at the Hoe Theatre in Plymouth. There were some big names in the company, including the famous pantomime dame George Lacey. This was Dave's first summer booking after leaving Butlins. Dave said that he used to earn two pounds, ten shillings for some gigs and it had usually cost him half of that to get to the venue wherever it was. Then he started to earn more, sometimes as much as five pounds a night. He did this for two years.

Dave Allen was getting his experience from all types of show, but he had not yet had the chance to pull up a stool and tell stories. He was still matching the audience's expectations of short one-liners or gags, fired off one after the other. He was to say in later years that some of these shows weren't shows at all, and he spoke of this time with a bitterness about how hard it had been and what little money he had earned.

But in 1959 he had had a taste of television and knew that this was the route to take. There was a lot of competition, though, from other comedians on television. It was too soon for Dave Allen in England.

Benny Hill had already achieved his first series on television running from 1955–57, so had Bob Monkhouse, Mike and Bernie Winters and Tony Hancock. There was a queue of quality performers waiting in the wings: Bruce Forsyth, Ken Dodd, Peter Cook, Dudley Moore, Stanley Baxter, Des O'Connor, Dave's friend Jimmy Tarbuck, the Two Ronnies and Morecambe and Wise. The television programmes were offering a different type of comedy apart from the headline act's own show.

There was a distinct shift in people's expectations from entertainers. Some acts survived the transition to television as, even though old-fashioned, they worked well. Puppet acts like Lamb Chop, Pinky and Perky, Topo Gigio, Lenny the Lion and ventriloquists like Ray Allen were very successful and endured for some years. Then the magicians like the legendary Tommy Cooper came into their own. Variety or club acts that wouldn't have been seen had they not been piped into people's homes, like Liberace and Danny La Rue, thrived on television.

The old radio hands were at their peak and venturing over from radio into television as well, for example Dickie Henderson, Michael Bentine and Arthur Askey. Some singer-entertainers were moving over, including Matt Munro and someone who would be very important to Dave Allen, Val Doonican. While all of these star acts had begun to develop their own style, there were a limited number of opportunities on the two television channels, BBC and ITV, for newcomers. But none of these names sat on a stool, smoked, drank and told five-minute-long stories. Dave Allen would have to wait for his opportunity.

Helen Shapiro had been a singing star at just fourteen years old. In June 1962, at sixteen, she topped the bill for a tour with Dave Allen 'the new young comedian' at the Hippodrome in Brighton. This was a big break for Dave Allen. He was on tour with a star and out of the club circuit and being paid properly for it.

They were performing twice nightly at 6.15 and 8.30 p.m., which would have been exhausting, alongside Martin Grainger's puppets, 'The Big Noise' George Eaton, The

Rocking Red Price Combo, The Hillsiders, Gary Miller and compèred by Clifford Davis. There were overnight journeys to the next 'gig' or venue, and when they arrived at each place, their day would be taken up finding their 'digs', grabbing something to eat and then rehearsing and soundchecks at the venue.

In 1963 the Helen Shapiro tour was joined by the Beatles, at The Granada in Bedford, and they started a tour around the UK. Dave took over the role of compère from Clifford Davis. They did a gruelling one-night-stand tour of thirty dates around the country, visiting Doncaster, Oxford and many others. The Beatles had returned from Berlin and had just released the album *Please Please Me* following the success of the single of the same name in January 1963.

Although a year before the first pirate radio station, Radio Caroline, began broadcasting in 1964, there was an air of rebellion and the notion that boundaries were being moved, and the feeling was that if you were under twenty, then you ruled the world. The expression 'You've never had it so good' was about to be absorbed into everyday conversation. Dave Allen, on tour with the 'Fab Four', the Beatles, was at the centre of it all.

Laurie Boynton, a Redcoat from Filey, remembers seeing Dave on tour with the Beatles. 'I saw Dave Allen when he was at Bedford. Some of the Redcoats were asked to do a "Beavers tour" all round the UK in the winter. It was for all the kids who had stayed at Butlins in the summer. Billy Butlin was clever like that. He made all the kids join up so that they would pester their parents into letting them see the shows round the country during the winter months. It was a great way of generating income during the off season for us Redcoats as well.

'The Granada [cinema], Bedford, was a great barn of a place seating over two thousand people. Well, we did the "Beaver" show that morning knowing that most of the audience were young girls who had sneaked in and were waiting for the Beatles.

'I stayed on after our show to watch Dave Allen as he was the compère and I wanted to see how Johnny's little brother was doing. When he came on to the stage, you couldn't hear a word of what he was saying. I thought that he really had some guts to go out on stage before all of those screaming girls. I remember thinking what a terrible job he had. They weren't listening to anything he said, and he was introducing some great acts like Kenny Lynch, but they all just ignored him and screamed.'

During this tour with the Beatles, they played the New Theatre in Oxford, and it was performing in Oxford that would turn out to be a catalyst in his career. Although Dave said at interviews that it was the larger-than-life singer 'Big Mamma' Sophie Tucker who had told him to try Australia, it isn't actually clear if she did indeed prompt him. Dave said that this had been while he was on tour in South Africa in 1962 or 1963 with her, but there are no records of this. (Ken Pitt, Sophie Tucker's press representative in the UK, said he had no recollection of any tour with Dave Allen and Sophie in 1962 or 1963, or indeed at any point during the forty years when he was working with Frank Sinatra or Sophie.) Although there is a story about a young British comic running over his allotted slot on one of her Dominion tours, this was not Dave Allen. Coincidentally, though, she is reported to have said to this unfortunate young man that he would be better off performing in Australia – in other words anywhere other than where she was, as she had been forced to cut some of her act to accommodate his mistake.

What is known is that at one of the Beatles shows an agent 'spotted' Dave Allen and offered him a tour of hotels and nightclubs. It didn't take a lot to persuade this talented Irishman that he should seek fame and fortune in Australia. Within days Dave Allen was on his way to the other side of the world. It was a long way from his family, his mother and brothers, but he must have sensed that it was the right thing to do.

As he headed off to Heathrow, having waved goodbye to the four Beatles, Helen Shapiro, his mother and Johnny, he may have dreamed of becoming a star, but he would have no idea how quickly he would realise this dream.

CHAPTER THREE

THE BOOMERANG COMEDIAN

In 1963, Dave Allen took a BOAC flight that stopped everywhere on the way to Sydney, including Rome, Baghdad, Karachi, Calcutta, Rangoon and Singapore. He had three days to think about his career and the life-changing move he was making. Later on he would also use these interminably long flights to build on his repertoire, with his tales of 'metal tubes full of farts' and the oxygen mask with the instructions that read 'in the event of the oxygen masks being dropped, place the mask over your face and breathe normally' – 'You're in a nose dive from thirty thousand feet and they tell you to breathe normally!' – and probably the most famous: the apparent lunacy of giving everyone a whistle to blow when you have ditched in the middle of the Atlantic Ocean – 'Sixty-feet-high waves, and they give you a whistle. Who on God's earth is going to hear you blowing that whistle?'

Over the years he was going to do this long-haul commute

between Australia and London hundreds of times. Luckily, over the years the journey was going to get shorter, by two days.

He arrived in Sydney at 8.30 a.m. alone. Even for an affable, talented, young Irishman, arriving in a new country thousands of miles away from home was not going to be easy. Of course he wasn't the first British comic to visit Australia – Morecambe and Wise sent Christmas greetings to everyone in 1958 via *The Stage* to all their fans from Sydney.

Dave Allen began a season at a small hotel in Sydney called The Chevron. He was performing in the Silver Spade Room as a support act to the Wagnerian soprano Helen Traubel. She liked Dave's work but suggested to him that he try a more relaxed approach and stopped doing his American-style corny one-liners. She thought he would do better if he told stories based on reality – of what had happened to him in his life. Dave listened to her and gradually reverted to the style of storytelling that he had learned from his father and began to evolve the act that would make him a star in Australia and England.

In the meantime, though, there would be hours of monotony and routine for a man who claimed to have found the job by accident. It was a calm beginning for the comic who later would be banned from appearing live on Australian television for two years.

From the Chevron he started a tour across Australia playing hotels and clubs. Touring away from home always sounds glamorous to people outside the entertainment industry. Partners and friends accuse you of being on holiday.

They get envious that you are staying in fabulous locations. Sometimes the reality can be far different: arriving in towns late at night, trying to find your 'digs', or hotel, in a strange place and traditionally in the pouring rain. There is never anywhere open to eat. On a very tough tour you might only ever see the venue and the hotel, the sights of the city taken as snapshots viewed through the window of a cab. Then, on the day of the show you have to occupy yourself walking, looking round, window shopping, 'doing' the art galleries and museums and, on a long tour, staving off boredom and loneliness. As a young man used to touring with the Beatles or Al Page, it would have been quite a culture shock to be totally alone, but for Dave Allen, it was an opportunity to start drawing and painting, something that everyone who worked with him in Australia remembered.

His first television appearance was in Melbourne on a programme called *In Melbourne Tonight*. Geoff Harvey, who was music director for the Nine television network for forty years, describes the show: 'He was extremely funny. He leapt on to the desk and did a whole pantomime; this was unheard of. Nobody had ever seen that.'

From Melbourne he returned to Sydney and was booked to appear at Chequers nightclub. 'This was a very different venue to the Silver Spade, not high-class at all; we would have said that its clientele were "racing identities", colourful characters, including criminals and crooks,' remembers Richard Lyle from Channel Nine. 'The police often turned a blind eye to the licensing laws and frequented the place themselves. Dave would perform for about forty-five to fifty minutes. It was a proper nightclub with dancing and dancers, but I always thought that it was a potential death trap with hundreds of people squeezed in there and what could have happened if there had been a fire. Sammy Wong who owned the place used to import big names, such as Lisa Minnelli and Shirley Bassey.'

Patrick Condon, a friend of Dave's for nearly forty years and executive producer of his television shows in Australia, remembers, 'The first time I met him he was appearing at Chequers nightclub, on the corner of Liverpool and Pitt Street in Sydney. The impresario, Jack Neary, had booked him.

'Jack Neary was a fascinating character. He was an ex-policeman who had been knocked down while doing points duty and had to stop being a copper. At the time Dave was living in a studio apartment in the Kings Cross area of Sydney, in Maclay Towers. For some reason he never opened the windows, and I used to call him a "Pommie idiot".

'I didn't know then that this young man, Dave Allen, would be my closest friend for some forty years. Even now that he his dead, I still find myself thinking, "I wonder what Dave would tell me to do," when I have a problem. I was so used to phoning him up, berating him and joking with him. He was so good at advice and help.

'At Chequers, Dave was either the mid or second comic. Jack had invited Bruce Grinshall from Channel Nine to come and see him. There was a lot of competition between Sydney and Melbourne, and in those days there was no satellite or network link so the television companies had to operate independently of each other.'

The 'other' city, Melbourne, had its own comic, Graham

Kennedy. Kennedy's style was based on innuendo. He was an intensely private man who allegedly made millions and spent them. On his appearances on *In Melbourne Tonight* Kennedy would tell stories from a different reality. He made slagging off the sponsor's products an art form. There are very few tapes of any performances by Graham Kennedy as all of his broadcasts were live and the stories of his appearances are reliant on people's memories, but Graham Kennedy didn't go down well in Sydney; they didn't like him at all.

In 1963 Sydney had found its own comic, Dave Allen. When Dave had made his first appearance on UK network television in 1959, it was just six years old. In Sydney television was two years old. (Although television started in Australia in 1956 in Melbourne to coincide with the Olympics, it didn't reach Sydney until a few years later.)

Geoff Harvey said, 'Dave arrived in Sydney, and it was all very low key. Nobody knew very much about television in those days. I think even Dave was ho-hum about the whole thing. But he decided, yes, all right, I'll give it a go. So in a sense you were making things up as you went along in terms of developing comedy or programming. Certainly from my side we were making things up. We would say, "What will we do this year?" – well, musically that's exactly what we did, but Dave Allen knew exactly where he was going. He knew he could be very funny. If anything, and I may be being a bit radical, I don't think we gave a stuff about what the television people thought, or what anyone thought.

'When Dave arrived in Sydney, I remember talking to him

and being struck by how completely different he was to any-one I'd ever seen. He wasn't show business; he was calm, gentle. The rest of them were, you know, "Hey, how are ya?" – loud, what people would call "in your face" nowa-days, that kind of thing. There was none of that; he was very gentle. We sat and discussed how we would do things and just calmly worked it all out.

'I don't think Dave realised how huge he was going to end up. We did the shows and they were very funny, extremely funny. He used to tell stories, certainly, but he didn't tell stories like everyone else. We were used to the one-liners. Dave didn't do "take my wife" jokes; he did lovely stories, gentle and completely irreverent and very funny. I was com-pletely amazed by the whole thing. We had very good peo-ple on television in those days, people like Bob Dyer [an American quiz-show host who became a household name in Australia with his wife, Dolly], people like that, but Dave was completely different with those stories.

'I can't remember any issues coming along, you know, where the compère threw tantrums to get his own way, no screaming down the corridors or that sort of carry-on. Dave just sort of quietly came in, did his thing, went home and worked on next week's show. He used to say, "If you don't like it, well, too bad. I'm not going to do a song," which was fine by me. I didn't want him singing and it didn't matter.'

The ratings began to reflect Dave's popularity. The buzz went round Sydney and viewers tuned in to see what the unpredictable Dave Allen would get up to. It became a late-night routine for the whole city to watch Dave Allen.

Bruce Menzies, who worked as an announcer on Dave's show, said, 'Dave's shows were radically different in that while each production had an intended shape, Dave set out to frustrate any formula and make each occasion an "original". Audiences wouldn't risk the chance of missing something extraordinary.'

Bruce Menzies continued, 'Australians are drawn to the larrikin [a likeable hooligan] element of our national character, and Dave, as a warm-hearted "wag", was able to deflate any whiff of pomposity and that met with great approval. While his humour took the mickey out of the establishment and pompous people, he did it entirely without malice. His stay was remembered for decades, and return visits were always a success. All over the world, no matter where I have been, Australians always come up to me and remember that I worked with Dave. I owe my television identity to Dave, and I have been ever grateful.'

The format of the shows in Australia was very different to the ones that were first broadcast in the UK. Patrick Condon, the executive producer and a friend of Dave's, said, 'When he did the first *Tonight with Dave Allen*, you could see he had a great raw talent. He did a combination of gags, one-liners, his rambling stories and he interviewed people. Dave also had a very dark side, and he went out of his way to find really strange people.

'Sydney has some deadly insects that are everywhere in the city. They are truly lethal, and Dave had a fascination about things like that. He once found this strange woman to interview who bred funnel-web spiders, which can kill you. He really liked all that chilling stuff. He liked the danger.

He went out of his way to find these weird people and to put himself in danger, but I don't think he gave the danger any thought at all.

'One night we had this guy on with all these Taipan snakes, which again are killers. During the interview the handler got one of the snakes out of the box and was showing it to Dave, and the audience loved it. Well, during the interview, while Dave was concentrating on the conversation and the snakes, which were right beside him, we dropped a rubber snake down on to Dave's lap from out of the grid. The audience screamed, and Dave was horrified. He leapt out of his seat, but he had to be so careful because he was so close to the real thing. It was very funny, and the audience loved it of course. Dave loved all those sorts of pranks and jokes.

'The audiences liked him because he was so innovative and it was pure instinct. One night we had the trampoline world champion on the show. Of course, Dave had to have a go. He got on the trampoline in his suit and was bouncing up and down and bounced straight off and on to the concrete floor. He landed straight on his head and knocked himself out.'

Geoff Harvey, the music director for the show, continued the story, 'I remember thinking, "God, now what do we do?" and I said to my trumpet player, "We should give him a brandy." And just by luck in the trumpet player's case there happened to be a bottle of brandy. One of the guys went across and gave him a swig when he came to, so it was all right.'

Patrick Condon and Neil Swanson took him to the

casualty department at the hospital and were teasing him that he did it to get a couple of days off. The doctors told Pat Condon that 'Nothing could damage that skull.'

Geoff Harvey continues, 'The tag to the story was that when the boss of the station, Ken Hall, was told about the brandy, he called me up and said, "That musician had liquor on the station, sack him immediately." That was the way they thought, but none of us really gave a stuff, so I said, "All right, but I think you're being very silly, but if that's what you want, fine." I didn't do anything about it of course. Well, the next day it was, "Now, Geoff, you make sure everyone knows the rules," but it wasn't enforced. The trumpeter kept his job and Dave was fine.'

The stories about his Australian shows came back to his friends in England but to no one else. He was still virtually unknown. Rocky Mason heard about how he handled advertising products live on air: 'Brett Cresswell, a Brit who went over to Australia to work for Australian television, told me how Dave won over the Australian viewers. They had live advertisements on the programmes, so every fifteen minutes the show would stop and Dave Allen would "sell" an item that was part of the commercial break. One of the first items was a Japanese radio. I think it is fair to say that the Australians really didn't like the Japanese after World War Two, so when this guy handed Dave a Japanese radio, live on television, Dave pushed the button and said, "Look, it doesn't even work. Japanese rubbish," and threw it off the set, in front of all those people. The audience loved it.'

Patrick Condon continued, 'He really was the first person to instinctively develop and have fun with the commercial break. The breaks were live and usually someone from the company handed the product to Dave for him to show the audience. Geoff Griffiths was the sales manager for Ronson shavers at the time, and we were presenting his "unbreakable shaver". Geoff was sitting with us up in the boardroom [the green room] when Dave was handed this shaver, live on air.

'None of us realised that Dave had hidden a hammer behind the table. When he was presented with the "unbreakable shaver", he just looked at the camera and the audience and cool as you like said, "Oh, unbreakable, is it?" and thwacked it with the hammer. It was an exploding mess of springs, foils, bits of plastic. They just flew off everywhere. We were all in hysterics, and I looked at Geoff Griffiths, who was holding his head in his hands, looking as though his life had collapsed and he was muttering, "I am finished." Of course Dave knew that the audience would love all this, and sales of the razor went through the roof. He could always spot the opportunity, and sponsors and advertisers were quick to get Dave to plug their products in his show.'

Dave's sense of humour and his fondness for pranks grew in Australia. Patrick Condon said, 'Dave did terrible tricks to people as well. Bruce Menzies was host and newsreader. One day Dave put eggs in his jacket pockets live on camera, and when he was reading the next announcement, he patted the pockets to make the eggs break, and Bruce had to carry on as if nothing had happened.'

Geoff Harvey said, 'Dave loved this country. In those days, unlike now, there was no real pressure. No one gave a stuff, and everyone had a great time. We didn't care if the show collapsed next week. We would have just said, "Oh well, what else can we do?"

'There were no network people laying down the law, telling us when to have commercial breaks, so it was lovely. And that's what Dave was like, very laidback, and in those days Australia was more laidback than it is today.'

People were by now becoming more aware of his versatility as a performer. He was not only an interviewer and a comic, but he was also an observer of people. They were amazed at how this comic could suddenly become so serious mid-interview.

Dave's fame was gathering momentum in Australia, and he took every opportunity to keep his name in the press. The journalists found it frustrating, though, that he really didn't have anything to tell them. He wouldn't discuss his background or his private life. There was a feeling that he rung them up to arrange interviews in order to have some company in his tiny flat. While the journalists thought that he had nothing to say, he still made it into the papers and kept his name in the public eye even when they weren't watching the shows.

In October 1963 the legendary singer Eartha Kitt appeared on Dave's show. Eartha Kitt smouldered at the good-looking young Irishman and the rumours started, probably helped by Dave himself to keep the media attention going. Dave was even reported to have told a news reporter that they were 'going steady'.

The papers were full of this 'romance', even telling people that Dave Allen had plans to go Hollywood to see her. 'No, none of that was true. Johnny told me that it was just a publicity stunt,' said Rocky Mason.

At Christmas 1963 Dave flew back to England, but this was a very different Dave Allen to the young comic who had made just one brief appearance on *New Faces*. He was a successful Australian television star and an experienced television performer.

Dave Allen was delighted to be back in London. He was able to see his mother and find out what his brother, Johnny, was doing and how his work was going at Butlins. This visit was a big opportunity for Dave in England; he was to appear on the highly successful television show *Sunday Night at the London Palladium*, and he would be appearing with some friends of his, the Beatles.

The London Palladium had a fabulous history as the home of variety in London, and in 1945 Val Parnell took over. Parnell was one of the most powerful people in the world of variety. When theatres were closing all around the country, Parnell invested in bringing over stars from the US to make the London Palladium the home of variety.

When ATV was born, Sunday was a crucial night for the ratings war on UK television. ATV London produced one of the longest-running shows, *Sunday Night at the London Palladium*. Tommy Trinder hosted the first show in 1955. The high-kicking Tiller Girls were a regular feature, as was the end sequence when all the stars and the Tiller Girls sat or stood by the famous 'London Palladium' letters as they went round on the huge revolving stage.

The revolve caused many problems. Judy Garland was too

'emotionally upset' to use it, and the Rolling Stones refused to appear on it as it didn't 'fit their image'. One night a power cut forced Tommy Trinder to ad-lib for two hours. When the power was restored and broadcast was resumed, he opened with 'Welcome to Monday morning at the London Palladium.'

Before Dave Allen would get his chance to compère the show, he would be preceded by Hughie Green, Dickie Henderson, Norman Vaughan, Roger Moore, and Bruce Forsyth. At its peak twenty-eight million viewers tuned in to watch it, which at that time was half the population of the United Kingdom. The London Palladium was the home of the first ever televised Royal Variety Performance.

While gaining him some valuable experience and the possibility of people spotting him, it would take a lot more than one appearance on this famous show to vault Dave Allen into the rising star category.

Dave Allen's first appearance on this stellar platform was just a short guest spot, and he was advertised as 'Dave Allen, The Irish American'. 'I thought he was dreadful,' Rocky Mason said. 'He did the whole act in an American drawl. He was obsessed with Lenny Bruce at the time and was doing a crude imitation of him. Luckily, when he returned to do the series, he was back to himself.'

Unbeknown to Dave, however, some very important people had spotted his talent; Bill Cotton and Lew Grade had watched the 'Irish American' and would remember him when he finally returned to England.

He flew back to Australia in January 1964 and returned to his series with Channel Nine. The character of this series remained the same with Dave interviewing his 'strange' or famous people. During this series he interviewed Emile Griffith, the middle-weight six-time world boxing champion.

Emile Griffith was renowned for having killed a man in the ring. His opponent, Benny 'The Kid' Paret, had started taunting him during the weigh-in about being gay. During the fight Emile had hit him under the instructions of his coach, 'fairly but consistently', and Benny 'The Kid' Paret had died.

Pat Condon remembered that 'the interview went very well, and Dave and I were invited to see Emile Griffith fight after the show. We enjoyed the fight, as Dave loved any sort of sport, and we were invited to the party afterwards.

'We went on to Emile's apartment in the ocean beach suburb of Bronte. It was an open-plan apartment, and at one end of the room was a large bed, which Dave and I went and sat on so that we were away from the mêlée of people.

'Emile spotted us and came over. He sat down beside Dave and started patting Dave's leg, saying how much he liked him. I thought that it was time to make my excuses, and I decided to let Dave handle this one on his own. It was very funny to watch Dave being "hit upon" by this huge boxer. I went over to the bar.

'Dave came over to find me afterwards to tell me that the boxer's manager had come over and dragged Emile away telling him, "Don't fuck with the talent." Dave was in hysterics. He loved all that sort of thing, bizarre or out of the ordinary situations; he liked to see what people would do and say.'

Like his father and brother, Dave loved to gamble, as Patrick Condon remembers: 'Dave loved sport, and it was a tradition with Dave, my son Michael and I that we had wagers on all sporting events. It didn't matter what it was – cricket, boxing, rugby, football, anything. Dave was hopeless; he always lost.

'Part of the whole game with Dave was that Michael would send letters with invoices to him for the money he owed. We wouldn't hear anything because Dave was waiting for the next "chapter" or letter. Then Michael would send a joke threatening letter, demanding payment. It was all part of the game.

'Every single time after a few weeks, a large brown paper parcel would arrive stuffed to the gills with afghani notes, or anything really unusual, hundreds of them. We used to be surrounded by these things. Then right in the middle would be two hundred pounds.

'What made us laugh even more was the thought of Dave Allen going to the bank in Kensington High Street and asking for all that unusual currency and then going to all that trouble of posting it. He adored jokes like that, and he would anticipate exactly what effect it would have on all of us.

'Last year, 2004, you may remember that there was a rugby World Cup. Dave said he would take a bet on it, and I was astonished: "What, you are betting on England winning?" And he said that no, he was betting on Australia losing. Now how Irish is that?

'Dave was an incredibly generous man. He just accepted people, rich or poor, and he stuck by you. My daughter, Simone, went over to stay with him a couple of years ago. It was only meant to be for a few weeks, but she stayed for two years. He didn't mind; he just said that he would "Get my own back later" and he would do, but it would be a joy; our two families were really joined by our friendship.'

In January 1964 Dave Allen interviewed a young actress, Judith Stott, on his show. Judith had a good reputation as an actress with the Royal Shakespeare Company and had appeared in several movies. She was starring in a play by Peter Shaffer at the time in Sydney, *The Private Ear and The Public Eye.* The young Dave Allen, miles away from home, was smitten with this intelligent, attractive, vivacious blonde. After a whirlwind romance, three months later on 9 March he married the divorced Judith, who had a son from her previous marriage, Jonathan. 'I remember that Richie Benaud, the Australian cricketer, who had just retired in 1964, was the best man,' Patrick Condon said.

But sadly, none of Dave Allen's family, his mother or brothers, had travelled all the way to Australia to see him get married. Rocky Mason said, 'I remember one of the Butlins Redcoats coming in to tell me that Johnny was packing up all his things. It was 1964 and we were in Bognor Regis. I went round to Johnny O'Mahony's room and was amazed to find him packing his suitcase. When I asked him what was going on, he told me that Dave had sent him his fare to join him in Australia. We were all thrilled for him. It was a terrific thing to be happening. I think he was going to sail there.

'A few weeks later the word went round the camp that Johnny was back in Bognor Regis. I went to see him and when I asked him what had happened, he just said, "You know what it is like. You have one drink to the old country, then one drink leads to another ..." and he just laughed and shrugged. I took this to mean that he had drunk the fare away.'

Intensely protective about his new private life, very few journalists knew that Dave had married, and within days of the wedding Judith was off on tour and returned to England, while Dave continued filming. There are few more demanding situations than two successful show-business personalities at opposite ends of the globe at the start of what they hope will be a long and happy marriage. The newlyweds were only too aware of the strains that would occur from communicating long-distance and the long, lonely periods of separation.

It was during 1964, just four years after leaving Butlins and turning professional, that Dave received the first award of his career. He was presented with a Logie for 'Most Popular Male', and the show, *Tonight with Dave Allen*, was voted the most popular programme.

For Dave Allen the rest of 1964 was spent on his television show and touring Australia. But he was very much on his own, and his time was spent waiting for the return of his new wife to Australia. Judith did come over to stay briefly then returned to England to carry on working. When Judith left again, Dave was faced with the agonising decision of whether to stay in Australia or return to England. He was torn between his success in Sydney and whether he should return to England to make his mark, settle down with Judith and see his mother and brothers.

He finally made up his mind to return to England. He was

going to leave a successful career and friends, but he knew that he would return to Australia soon. Back in England he would be with Judith and Jonathan, certainly, but he would have to start in earnest to build his career almost from scratch.

Geoff Harvey remembers when Dave told him that he was going home: 'He invited me over to his flat in Potts Point. He was fairly grotty, you know – he used to have toothpaste on his tie, nothing dreadful, but he was fairly grotty, and unmoved, and I went over there that afternoon, and he told me that he was going home. Dave said, "Look, Geoff, I'm going back to England, to London, to work, and why don't you come with me?"

'I was flattered, of course, but I explained that I was having a great time, it was fantastic in Australia. I was a big fish in a little pond, like Dave was. It was good of him to ask me, but I wasn't going to leave all this behind. I told Dave that I didn't think that England was ready for his kind of humour. Ha ha, that's me advising Dave Allen.

'Of course he went back and became so famous. I went back several times to England over the years, and whenever I saw him he would always say, "Do you remember telling me that I shouldn't come back?" What could I say other than "Hey, well, there you go, Dave."'

In December 1964 hoards of fans turned up in Sydney to wave goodbye to the Irish comic whom they would call an 'honorary Australian' in years to come. With his traditional champagne at 35,000 feet, he was saying goodbye, albeit temporarily, to fame and a good life in Australia.

Thrilled to be back home at their flat in Hampstead, Dave

and Judith had just a short time together before his career took him back on the road, touring clubs and venues all over England. From such a stellar beginning in Australia, he was now starting again, creating his own niche among the competition in the UK. The comic scene in England was moving quickly, and for Allen the touring circuit of clubs and small theatres was a far cry from the successful life he had worked for in Australia.

While Dave had been in Australia, another Irishman had been spotted on *Sunday Night at the London Palladium*, a singer called Val Doonican. Val was offered his own show on BBC television. This was a relaxed, easygoing show. Val Doonican had a trademark rocking chair; he sang good songs; there were some sketches and guests, and this gentle programme became another 'must see' for British television viewers.

Bill Cotton, head of variety for the BBC, had spotted Dave on his appearance at the Palladium. Bill Cotton asked Val if he would go and see Dave Allen perform as he was sure not only that Val would like him, but that he would be perfect for the show. Cotton thought that the two Irishmen would complement one another and the programme would have a good balance. John Ammands, a BBC producer, was sent to see Dave Allen appear at a club near Newcastle and he remembered, 'I liked Dave immediately, but I did have a big concern. We were looking at a show with Val that ran for eleven weeks or editions. I wasn't sure before I saw him that Dave Allen would have enough material for eleven appearances of five minutes each. That is a lot of material.

'I didn't realise of course that just one of his stories could last five minutes so appearing for eleven editions and being able to come up with the content would not be a problem.

'Val and Dave did get on very well. I used to meet with Dave a couple of days before the show, at his flat in Hampstead where he lived with his charming wife, Judith, and her son, Jonathan. If ever I phoned him to call him in for a rehearsal, he used to joke that I was "interrupting" his sex life. He was such a nice young man. The Val Doonican shows were broadcast live from the BBC TV theatre in Shepherds Bush.

'One day Dave told me at our pre-show script meeting that he was going to do the Irish take on funerals. He always had dark humour about things like that. It would have been very funny. Sadly, though, we had just had a dreadful disaster in a Welsh village called Aberfan. This was on Friday 21 October in 1966. It was awful; one hundred and sixteen children alone had been killed when this hill of coal waste had slid down and swamped the local school and some houses.

'The funeral was in the week that Dave and I were meeting, and the country was in a very sad mood, and I told Dave that it wouldn't work, that it wasn't a good idea at all. He tried to persuade me that the Irish take on funerals would help everyone, but then he agreed with me. That was the only time I had to interfere with him.

'Val wouldn't have liked anything that was risqué, nor would I. I always thought that Dave was at his strongest and most successful when he kept away from anything with bad language in it.

Dave appeared on *The Val Doonican Show* on BBC1 for eleven editions from 7 October to 16 December. Dave Allen soon began to get his own following on the programme. He was offered a further series of six-minute slots with Val Doonican, and Lew Grade, the founder of ATV, had noticed him.

John Ammands continued, 'We tried to get him to do another series, but we got the feeling that he didn't want to be overexposed, at least that is what his agent told us. He did do a few more odd slots but not another whole series as we would have liked.'

'Bill Cotton was very anxious to sign Dave up for the BBC. He didn't want to lose Dave to the opposition, ITV. He really did pursue him,' remembers James Moir, who went on to be head of light entertainment. 'Dave was a very good-looking young man, which was so unusual for a comic. They usually trade on whether they are fat, thin, bald, whatever. With that glass of Scotch and his cigarette he had what could only be described as machismo. Combine all that with his remarkable talent and you had a very unusual young man. Bill Cotton got Dave to do a pilot for a comedy programme called *The Early Show*. This had Dave as the interviewer and raconteur, which of course he was tremendous at, and Bill had found some bizarre guests for that pilot.

'There was a man called Butty Sugoo, who was an Irishman who had a pub and could pull motorcycles that were revving away along with his teeth. It was very weird. The other guest on this pilot was probably the reason why it never was broadcast. This guy was a champion egg swallower. He had dozens of eggs in a pint beer glass that he swallowed in one go. It was revolting to watch. One of the producers who was sitting at the back made his excuses to go to the gents rather than stay and watch. He was feeling very queasy. Of course the producer was using the gents when the egg swallower came in and regurgitated all the eggs in front of him. He would have been safer staying where he was.

'Bill Cotton was really upset that the pilot didn't work and that meant he would, after all, lose Dave to the "other side".'

At the end of his series with Val Doonican Dave was back touring, but at least one of his bookings was close to home and he would see Judith. He appeared at the successful Showboat Theatre and restaurant on Trafalgar Square in London. He also did a tour of Jewish venues and events.

Author Michael Freedland said, 'I remember seeing him at the Majestic Hotel in London. It was a Jewish event, so he walked on to the stage and said, "As you're all Jewish, I don't suppose there is any point in my asking for a Scotch and soda."

'I remember thinking that he was very funny, good-looking and saying as we all left, "My God, he's good."'

Dave explained that the reason he drank during the show stemmed from the days when he would 'bum' the odd drink in nightclubs when it was hot and he was broke. Then he found that people were offering him drinks he did not really like, such as gin and tonic or rum. So he decided to bring his own, and that is how the image of Dave Allen with the glass of Scotch became almost his trademark.

With Dave's television career in England beginning, 1966 marked a turning point too in the Allen's family life as Dave and Judith's first child together, Jane, was born. Judith's career would be put aside while she was at home with the baby, and she would watch her husband become a star. This strain would eventually tell on the marriage. 'Dave and Judith were absolutely besotted with each other,' remembers Patricia Smyllie.

In July, just a few months after Jane was born, possibly the biggest opportunity and compliment that could be offered to a performer in England came to Dave: Dave was to present *The Blackpool Show*, as the star of the show, comedian Tony Hancock, had been taken ill.

The show was highly successful not only because of Hancock but also because of the high calibre of guests. The show had been running for six weeks and included such stars as Kathy Kirby, Dave's friend the singer Matt Munro, Frankie Howerd and The Bachelors.

On 23 July Dave received a late-night call asking him if he would host the show for ITV the next day. He travelled from his home in Hampstead and got to Blackpool just in time for the show. He was completely unrehearsed, but he was so natural that no one could tell. His years of experience in Australia and on *The Val Doonican Show* took him out of the ranks of the new comedian and established him firmly in everyone's mind. (Tony Hancock came back for just one show on 31 July and then was replaced on the last show by Bruce Forsyth.)

Dave continued round the club circuit when not appearing on television, but there was a difference now; he had a following of fans who had seen him on television. Rocky Mason remembers, 'Dave used to ring me up and offer me gigs with him all over the south coast. He used to perform at the top-rank suites, for example in Brighton, but he topped the bill now. He was well known after Val Doonican and of course *The Blackpool Show*.

'One of my jobs was to make sure we had eight to ten glasses of whisky ready for the act. Of course he went on with one and an ashtray. About one hour and twenty minutes into the act he used to call me over and say, "Rocky, that table over there has been laughing a lot. Give them a drink, Rocky." So I used to hand out the whisky and empty his ashtray, do a bit of a routine with him that always got a laugh and exit quickly!

'He had started doing his religious gags by this stage. He had never done these at Butlins because of all the rules. There was a great one he told about a young guy who goes into the confessional. The priest was very forgetful and when the guy said that he had sinned, the priest said, "What have you done, my son?"

'The young guy told him, "Father, I have been intimate with a girl."

'The priest would make marks on the sleeve of his cassock with a piece of chalk for the number of sins this represented.

'"How many times have you done this dreadful thing, my son?" asked the priest.

'"At least four times," said the young man, and the priest marks his sleeve with more chalk marks.

'"Who is this poor girl?"

'"The vicar's daughter," replied the young man, and the priest rubs off all the chalk marks.

'"Don't worry, my son, that doesn't count."

'The audience use to love that one. They weren't used to someone joking about the Church at all. Dave used to ask for me to join him as he knew that I was trying to buy a house at the time and he always thought of me,' said Rocky Mason.

In September 1966 his success as a stand-in for Tony Hancock was rewarded with what promised to be the start of his own television series on ITV. The BBC would have to wait for him.

Dave recorded a pilot for a series called *Around with Allen*. Featuring Dave in a series of solo spots (written for him by Eric Merriman) with sketches (written by Alistair Foot and Tony Marriott) played by Patrick Cargill, Bob Todd, Arthur Mullard, Victor Maddern and Penny Ann France, the pilot was screened on 5 March, but it was only broadcast in the Midlands and the north of England and not in London or the rest of the UK. The network screening of Dave Allen was still to come. In the end ABC (one of the ITV television companies) decided not to take up the option to record a series and let Dave go.

In 1967 the now experienced and confident Dave Allen accepted the invitation of Sir Lew Grade and hosted *Sunday Night at the London Palladium*. Sir Lew Grade thought that Dave had a natural wit. He liked him as a person and thought that he was unique as he didn't try to be funny. He had what Grade thought was 'star quality'.

Everything moved very quickly for the thirty-year-old Allen from this point. The audiences warmed to his humour and his personality, and later that year his dream of starring in his own television series in England was realised. ITV broadcast thirteen episodes of *Tonight with Dave Allen* across the UK ITV network. This was a huge turning point in his career and established him as a television personality and household name. Just seven years after his first television appearance, this series was to win him the Variety Club's 'ITV Personality of the Year' award.

Full of quirky stories, that chair and some bizarre and wonderful sketches showing a different angle to life, the series was shown late on a Sunday night and would become the talking point in offices around the country the next day. (Series one ran from 9 July to 1 October.) Dave combined his short gags and rambling monologues with 'bizarre sketches' and 'turns by amateur eccentrics from the general public who were invited on to the studio floor'.

This series replaced the highly successful late-night slot that had been occupied by a fellow Irishman, Eamonn Andrews. *The Eamonn Andrews Show* went out at 11.05 p.m. on a Sunday night, and the critics watched carefully to see how Dave's success in Australia would be matched in the UK. They also thought that Andrews was a very hard act to follow, even for another Irishman. Dave Allen received mixed reviews, but the ratings grew nicely for a late Sunday night programme.

In December 1967 he was given the accolade of a Christmas special on ITV, broadcast on 23 December. Sir Lew Grade saw the effect that the show was having on the ratings and tried to persuade Dave to move from his late-night slot to a prime-time early evening slot in place of David Frost's successful *Frost on Saturday*. Grade thought this would be an obvious move for the intelligent Allen. Dave would get an even wider audience, younger viewers and would give the BBC something to worry about on a Saturday night. But Allen refused to budge from his late-night slot. His humour and style were set for an adult audience, and he felt comfortable with that. Grade was astonished at Dave Allen's response but relented, and his show stayed in its late-night Sunday slot.

This request from Lew Grade must have set Dave looking around for other opportunities, new challenges and perhaps even a change of television company.

In May 1968 Dave and Judith had a son, Edward. Judith's career was now very firmly in the background, but the rising star, Dave, started to work on his first BBC programme, *The Dave Allen Show*.

Bill Cotton had finally got his wish of getting Dave Allen on to the BBC. Broadcast on 8 June, this was a fifty-minute special 'in colour'. In a late-night slot on Sunday night, it suited Dave's style, and his audience were quick to follow him over to the BBC. The show was produced by Ernest Maxim, who was renowned for his work on large-scale events. Maxim was invited to work on the series with Dave.

Maxim started to help Dave Allen change his style. 'I liked Dave from the moment I saw him in the early sixties. My brother, Gerry, who had been a Redcoat with Johnny O'Mahony, took me to see him.

'I liked Dave immediately, before I had seen his performance. I think that is the true definition of star quality. You see lots of movie stars who cannot actually act very well, but you like them. Of course, Dave was very young then, but Gerry had said that I would like him and I did.

'When we started work together, I told him to slow down a little and to take his time. I noticed when he was sitting down, he slowed down and became very relaxed, so I suggested that he sat for his routines, and that's the start of the visual impact of Dave Allen and his chair. It suited the cameras and the television style so well. I told him to think about what he was saying, "brush some fluff off your collar if you need to, smooth your trousers, shift the focus, pull everyone in to you so that they listen to you", and it made a tremendous difference to him.

'He was very open to help. He was highly intelligent and had up to that point either been the interviewer on his Australian TV series or had "performed" as a comic. We needed to change that for his television shows.

'During rehearsals when we were working on the sketches and scenes, I told him to forget that he was a comic and start acting. It's a completely different mindset. It would allow people to see him, the real person, not Dave Allen the comic doing a funny sketch. At the beginning I think he was almost frightened to do this, to reveal who he was. But I told him that people or audiences need to like the performer. I would sit with him and talk through the scenes to bring out the real Dave Allen. I did the same with Morecambe and Wise when they first came into television. Like Dave, they were used to performing in vast theatres, but for television it is completely different. I got Eric and Ernie to pretend that they were working in a living room and it worked. They used smaller gestures and smaller voices which worked so well on television.

'When it came to doing the "takes" with Dave, I told him to do it exactly as he had done at the rehearsals and not to push it, in other words don't push for laughs. When the audiences started laughing he grew with the audience, and it grew that way, on the back of the applause. We had a live audience then and never used "canned laughter"; we didn't ever need to, especially not with Dave.

'I directed two series with Dave and really liked him. He had a tremendous sense of fun and could be quite a prankster. We were rehearsing just off Baker Street one day, with Matt Munro, Dave and Edward Woodward. There were lots of dancers as well. It was going to be a really large show. I got an unexpected call telling me that I had won the Charles Chaplin Award in Geneva for the Charlie Drake 1812 overture show that I had directed; it was the one where Charlie played everyone in the orchestra.

'Dave was delighted for me and said that this was such a great honour that we needed to go out at lunchtime and cele- brate. Matt, Dave, Edward and I went to the pub over the road for lunch. I am a teetotaller and never drank, but that day he said that it was such an occasion that I really should. Dave ordered four pints of Guinness and we stood drinking them, celebrating my success. I sipped a little, and we talked about the award. After about twenty minutes I noticed that my pint of Guinness hadn't gone down at all. Dave had been topping it up with champagne.

'I couldn't walk back to the rehearsal rooms. You can imagine what effect this had on me as I really didn't ever drink. Back in the rehearsal all the dancers were waiting for us, and they took one look at all of us and started laughing.

It was chaos, none of us could do anything for laughing, and I had to cancel the rehearsals for that day.

'He was an incredibly warm, even emotional man and superbly talented. There was one thing that I wouldn't let him do at the time and that was any religious gags or sketches. In a theatre it was fine to do that sort of thing. There are a thousand people all laughing and everyone joins in. On television you are a guest in someone's home, and if you offend them with a joke about religion, then they won't laugh and you have lost them.'

Following the special, the series of *The Dave Allen Show* was broadcast on Saturdays at 7.30 p.m. It was much earlier than he was used to and called for a different angle to his stories and sketches, which gained him a family viewing audience but meant he couldn't do the sketches or tell the sort of adult stories that he wanted to. The BBC was about to lose Dave Allen after just one series.

While he had been working with Ernest Maxim, Dave had also been hosting a show for ATV called *The Big Show*. Directed by Philip Casson and produced by Jon Scoffield, the guest stars included, Kathy Kirby, Frank Ifield and the Dave Clark Five. The series ran from April to July.

Dave Allen switched back to ITV, and on 29 September the second series of *Tonight with Dave Allen* was shown on Saturday nights, in his favourite late-night adult-viewing slot of 11.20 p.m., where his religious jokes and his favourite style of story could be told. The viewers again moved with him, and the series was a great success.

Always searching for new ideas and different angles for his interests and talents, in 1969 Dave Allen travelled to

New York to film *Dave Allen in the Melting Pot*, the melting pot being the huge city of New York. This could hardly have seemed like work for the man who took immense time and pleasure to speak to anyone, no matter who they were.

He used to say that most of his friends have no connection with his professional life. He called a lot of them 'tramps' and 'bums'. He thought that there was nothing strange in this because before he became famous that is exactly how he saw himself.

Dave spent the programme interviewing people who at that time were on the edge of conventional society and who most programme-makers of the time would have shied away from. He spent nine weeks in New York filming and speaking to all sections of society from alcoholics, men and women on skid row to police undercover squads, drug pushers' psychiatrists and extreme militant groups from all racial backgrounds. It was especially unusual for a stand-up comic of Dave's calibre to have tackled these sorts of interviews. But for him it was perfect. He was not only talking to people but watching and listening to them as well.

Well received on both sides of the Atlantic, this programme made television history as it featured Dave conducting the first ever broadcast interview with men who were openly gay.

The 1960s saw Dave Allen's career change in the UK from a struggling, ambitious but highly talented jobbing comedian to a recognised star, a household name in both the UK and Australia. His relaxed style made him stand out from the formulaic comics who did their one-liners, repeated their catchphrase and ended with a song. His own performance too had grown from the late fifties.

Here was an intelligent, driven performer, curious to find new and ambitious outlets for his talent, but still keen to maintain his roots on the club and performance circuits in England. He had not started to use the tougher religious material in his shows yet, or used any social commentary on politics or 'current affairs' either, because he was not allowed to due to scheduling restrictions. His channel-hopping between the BBC and ITV because of various disappointments or restraints was to become a feature of his television career in England.

CHAPTER FOUR

CONTROVERSY

The 1970s have always been considered to be when Dave Allen's fame was at its highest. He looked invincible. His shows were fast moving, irreverent and outrageous. Even when confronted by controversy either about language or religion, his popularity never really slumped in any way.

This was the decade that he spent being dumped in tanks of water and shot at behind bullet-proof glass; he took huge risks and pushed himself to the limit. He also ventured into writing, compiling a book, and 'straight acting'.

He was able to take risks with his sketches, specifically of course the religious ones, although they weren't always broadcast. Whenever this happened and decisions were made without him, he swapped channels to continue his work. He became adept at channel-hopping.

Always looking for that new challenge, Dave Allen returned to Australia in 1970, although only for a few weeks, to film the movie *Squeeze a Flower*. Shot on location in Hunter Valley and in Manly, Sydney, Dave was billed as 'Introducing Dave Allen'. Directed by Marc Daniels, written by Charles Isaacs and starring Walter Chiari, Rowena Wallace, Sue Lloyd and others, Dave played the role of Tim O'Mahony in this comedy about an Italian monastery and their precious recipe for their unique 'brew'. This made-for-television movie gained good reviews for Allen. He was back with his friends in Australia and in the best place possible to develop his love of red wine.

When Dave Allen left for Australia, England was just beginning a very bleak time. There wasn't a lot to laugh about, yet it was to be the peak of his fame and popularity on any television channel.

The seventies in the UK were about strikes and strife. Times were harsh. In 1970 a state of emergency was declared over the dockers' strike; the post workers who had been on strike returned to work in 1971. Then came the biggest and most controversial strike of all: the miners' strike in 1972. This strike brought with it power cuts, television blackouts and the three-day working week. Workers travelled to work with a variety of torches and candles, and on every high street in England shops were in darkness, save for hurricane lamps and an assortment of emergency lighting. It was also very cold. The blackouts and power cuts weren't restricted to any particular time of day or night; television programmes suffered, and people sat at home in the dark and shivered.

Somehow in between power cuts ITV/Thames managed to film *Inside the Mind of Dave Allen*. Shot on his return to England in July, this was a sixty-minute colour special. It was also broadcast in July, starring Dave Allen and Bob Todd and was produced by John Robbins. This was the beginning of his own unique style that was to mark him as a very different type of entertainer. He had abandoned telling the short gags on their own, and the gags were now used to start long, rambling tales. With a combination of Dave sitting telling his stories to camera and bizarre sketches, it was an instant hit.

Michael Sharvell-Martin, who appeared with Dave on *Inside the Mind of Dave Allen*, remembered a new series that was aborted. 'There is also a whole series that you won't find any record of. We had just done *Inside the Mind of Dave Allen*, and Thames Television offered him a series. It was a nightmare. I had never seen Dave lose his temper. Of course, like everyone, he got stressed when we were on deadline and focused on the end result, but this was so unlike him, and the whole thing was a sorry experience. We were all just in the wrong place at the wrong time and with the wrong people. They did record some of it, but it was never broadcast.

'So off we all went back to the BBC. Peter Whitmore phoned me and asked, "Why has Dave scribbled in the margin of the script, 'Four fucking hours just to film this.'" I told him that it was too long a story to go into and to ask Dave.'

By this time Dave Allen was a very bankable product, and he knew it. He discovered quickly that it didn't matter which channel he appeared on, as the other 'side' would always be vying for him and the ratings that came along with him. It allowed him an escape route when a show or programme was not going his way or something upset him about the end result.

Although unusual, he was not the first performer to discover that after a long association with a particular channel it was not career-threatening to move, something that both Michael Parkinson and Bruce Forsyth discovered in more recent years.

Peter Vincent and Ian Davidson were two of the core team of writers, with Austin Steele, for the BBC Dave Allen series *Dave Allen at Large* in the 1970s (and on into the two series in the eighties and nineties). A total of thirty-three episodes of this series were shown throughout the seventies on BBC2, except for one special that was broadcast on BBC1. They were shown just on the watershed, at 9.30 p.m.

This series marked the start of the familiar combination of monologues by Dave and extravagant sketches on the BBC.

With a host of writers, it would be easy to envisage a room full of creative minds and laughter through the script meetings, but the work behind the scenes to create the Dave Allen shows, in any of their guises, was a fascinating process, as Peter Vincent remembers: 'We all used to sit round a table with Dave and come up with ideas, sometimes lines, sometimes just words, but Dave would give you nothing back. He would actually sit there looking quite grim about it all. There were no laughs during these script meetings. It probably would have been totally unlike anyone would have imagined.

'Dave would sometimes just drift off, walk out of the

room, then come back twenty minutes later and either all or nothing of our suggestions would be included. Not that it mattered; it was part of the process, but he was very strange like that. After lunch Austin and Dave would just drift off to sleep, leaving me just sitting there. It was usually caused by a bottle of champagne at lunch!

'He could really be quite odd. Sometimes he would just forget that he had meetings arranged, and when we caught up with him the next day, he wouldn't ever have a reason for why the meeting hadn't happened; he would just shrug.

'Making a television programme, especially comedy, is extremely hard work. Everyone gets tense. Dave hated having a script. He always wanted to appear "off the cuff". So we had these huge "idiot cards" that had eight to ten key prompt words on them. I would sit during the rehearsals and the filming holding these things up for Dave. I never knew where he was in the story. We would use about twenty of these cards during one show. Sometimes he would miss out words three or four and I would then be left wondering whether he was going to go back to them or on to words six and seven.

'He would do a head jerk at me to indicate when to change. What was fascinating was that he never did the same thing twice. That's why those shows were so remarkable because he appeared so laidback.

'With Dave, though, the final editing process was very easy as he always gave you about forty-five minutes more than you actually needed so you weren't ever scrabbling around for material. It is a terrific shame that they have not re-run the *At Large* series.'

Valerie Wilson was a producer's assistant and worked in Michael Hurll's office, opposite Austin Steele's. 'I used to go to Dave's house for the day to type up his ideas and scripts straight from the horse's mouth. He would always cook us a great lunch, and then we would take a walk in Holland Park or Kensington Gardens, and Dave would keep wild-flower seed and grass seed in his pocket to scatter anywhere along the way.

'There was always a twinkle in his eye, and he was very relaxed in company that he knew and trusted.'

Actress Jacqueline Clarke first met Dave in 1971, when she was chosen to work on the series with him. Dave Allen collected an ensemble of actors who would stay with him for some years. Jacqueline Clarke was joined by Michael Sharvell-Martin and Sabina Franklyn.

Jacqueline Clarke remembers, 'I had been working in a pub in Hampstead doing some music-hall acts. The writer Alan J.W. Bell spotted me and told Peter Whitmore, a pro-ducer at the BBC, about me. I was thrilled to get the job. Dave was an incredibly attractive man, which seemed to make me very nervous. He was very kind and gentle. Whenever he spoke to you, he made it seem as if you were the only one that mattered at that moment, which is an art.

'I had a very useful "look" for comedy: I could blend in anywhere. Dave used to joke about me that it took me three hours in make-up to look beautiful but just give me a hat and I could play an old bag! He used to do "off-the-cuff" sketches when he would just grab me, get me to put on a

tatty hat, tell me to sit beside him in the car and begin ranting on at him, nagging him. It was completely unscripted,
then he would open the sunroof on the car, and we would
drive over a humpback bridge and I would go flying out of
the sunroof mid-gag.

'When we started in 1971, he focused on historical
sketches, for example I played Guinevere and then
Cleopatra. Of course the gag with Cleopatra was that
I dropped my Asp, the snake, down my front and had to
grapple to get it back. He was very clever at twists in
the stories.

'Then came the religious gags, and he had a fixation about
the confessional box. We did so many sketches set in and
around the confessional. There was lunacy as well, with
nuns on trolleys and things like that. Of course there were
things that weren't aired that had just either gone too far or
just didn't work.'

Michael Sharvell-Martin remembers filming in the familiar red cloaks worn during the 'Pope' sketches. 'You could
tell how long we had been filming by the state of the red
cloaks; if we had a damp mark around our chest we had
been standing there since the morning. They were dreadful
things that just sucked up water.'

Michael continued, 'I appeared on *Benny Hill*, then I got
the chance to do *Inside the Mind of Dave Allen*. It was the
start of a twelve-year working relationship with Dave and a
long-term friendship. I describe working on all the Dave Allen
shows as being allowed to play with the biggest dressing-up
box in the world, called the BBC, and being paid to do it.
The wardrobe staff were incredible. Dave would wake up

and tell them he had just had a great idea for a sketch, and they would have to rustle up the costumes from whatever they had with them at the time. One sketch about a Japanese prisoner of war was particularly challenging for them as we were filming on a Sunday with no shops open. They grabbed a pair of someone's striped pyjama trousers and twenty minutes later a costume appeared.

'Dave had a love of the Edwardian era and was fascinated by their fixation about flying machines. He created this sketch where Jacqueline and I were obviously lovers, but we had these beautiful feather wings, like the old flying enthusiasts used to try and fly. Jacquie and I did this mating dance with the wings in full Edwardian garb; it was very charming.

'Dave was quiet, reflective, down-to-earth. His generosity as a performer was incredible. If we were out on location and it was taking hours for him to change make-up from one character to another, he would say to Peter Whitmore, "Get Michael or one of the others to do it – I don't mind." And he really didn't mind, because he reasoned that even if someone else was very funny on the show, it still said "Dave Allen" on the title so it meant that everyone benefited. He was definitely the star, but as everyone will have told you by now, he never behaved like one. It was like a team. Not many comics would let someone else get the laughs.

'He was also a prankster. We were filming a sketch of Irish pirates digging for treasure, but the gag was that we were in the sea not on the shore and we were up to our waists in water and freezing. Dave looked warm and comfortable, and of course we discovered that he had a wetsuit

The Old Mill House in Keenagh where the Tynan O'Mahonys lived in 1941. (*Regina Lavelle*)

The school in Keenagh that Dave Allen attended in 1941.

Dave Allen's drawing of his father which hangs in The Knocklyon Inn. (*Regina Lavelle*)

Dave Allen as a Redcoat at Butlins in Brighton. (*Special collections, Auckland City Libraries*)

Dave Allen on tour with The Beatles and Helen Shapiro. (*The Badger Press*)

Dave on his first appearance on *Sunday Night at the London Palladium*. (*Phil Warren Archives*)

Dave Allen in *Squeeze a Flower*. (*Ronald Grant Archive*)

Michael Sharvell-Martin dressed for a more serious role in a Dave Allen episode.
(*Michael Sharvell-Martin*)

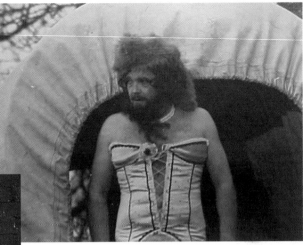

Dave Allen rehearsing for Peter Pan with Maggie Smith in 1973. (*PA/Empics*)

Dave Allen, leading Michael Sharvell-Martin, Jacqueline Clarke and others off to work. (*Michael Sharvell-Martin*)

Dave Allen on stage in Christchurch, New Zealand. (*Phil Warren Archives*)

Judith Stott, Dave Allen's first wife. (*Ronald Grant Archive*)

'Dave Allen gave me this lovely drawing of a badger that he had done in Devon. The verse is very Dave Allen.' Jacqueline Clarke.

Dave Allen on stage at the Albery Theatre in London. (*PA/Empics*)

Dave Allen signing copies of his book, *A Little Night Reading*, at Ye Olde Cheshire Cheese on Fleet Street. (*AP/Ampics*)

Dave Allen with Judy Garland. (*Special Collections, Auckland City Libraries*)

'Dave was so cross with me for forgetting his suit. I explained that we had the journey from hell overnight and then took this picture of him in his underpants in the Star Dressing Room, complete with graffiti on the breeze blocks and luxurious plastic chair.' Michael Condon.

Cilla Black, Dave Allen and Ruby Wax at the British Comedy Awards in 1996. Dave received a lifetime achievement award. (*Empics*)

Dave Allen with his wife, Karin Stark. (*Ireland on Sunday*)

'We thought we had been so clever coming up with this present for Dave but he never mentioned it.' Jacqueline Clarke. (*Michael Sharvell-Martin*)

on underneath his pirate's costume. He was fine and we were all freezing.

'I suppose that I was just as bad. We were filming this huge French Revolution sketch with soldiers, peasants, guillotines and carts. I was playing a hunchback executioner. Dave was playing someone about to be beheaded. As I dragged him up to the guillotine and got him to kneel ready to lose his head, I whispered in his ear, "I suppose a fuck's out of the question?" Well, Dave just collapsed, and of course Peter Whitmore went nuts because of the time-wasting. Every time we went for a take as Dave knelt down we both just went again. Happy memories.

'Later on I noticed that he changed his act. It became very angry and a little basic, which didn't really reflect what he could do. There were a lot of letters of criticism to the BBC, but he was confident about what he could do.'

Actress Jacqueline Clarke said, 'He always surprised us with the other side of him. He was living down in Devon, in Lynmouth. He had a big house down there and watched all the wildlife. He gave me a lovely sketch of a badger. He used to sit and watch them and sketch them. He was really very gentle.

'We used to get into so much trouble with the giggling that went on on-set. There was a sketch where I was stripped of my Air Force uniform by the RSM, and of course I ended up in stockings and suspenders, and you can see everyone giggling even on the take of the sketch. It was hopeless.

'Dave never stopped working on the script and developing it. Peter Whitmore, the producer, knew that I liked time to learn a complicated script. We were doing a sketch of the end of the world, and Peter told me that I had pages to learn but that I had a fortnight to learn it. I was very grateful of course to have this time.

'On the coach down to Docklands for the filming, I noticed that Dave was being very uncommunicative and scribbling away. We got out of the coach and Dave handed me sheets and sheets of scribble. When I asked him what it was, he calmly said that the other script had been "rubbish" but not to worry, "just get the drift of the script and let's see what happens". I thought he was sending me up, but he was serious. Amazingly we did it in one take.

Peter Whitmore, who produced *Dave Allen at Large* and *Dave Allen* for the BBC, was at the receiving end of the jokes and the hard work. He remembers, 'Dave didn't want to be the centre of attention, no showing off, if you like. He was highly professional. When you compared him to Terry Scott, whom I was working with at the time, Terry was "on stage" the whole time. He was actually very nice but loud, if you like. But Dave reminded me more of June Whitfield – professional, thoughtful and producing the goods when you wanted them. You knew he was quietly getting on with the job. I got a lot from working with Dave; it was a very pleasant way to earn a living.

'One of the sketches or jokes that managed to slip by was one in which Dave was dressed as a bishop. He was reading from an enormous Bible with an altar boy standing beside him. As he reached the end of the reading, the boy slammed the Bible shut, and you could see from Dave's expression exactly which bit of his anatomy had been caught in the book. He screamed in a high-pitch voice, "Amen."

'Well, we took the sketch out of the show on the instructions of Bill Cotton, who thought it too near the mark. I waited for a while, in fact it was when all the BBC top brass were all safely at the BAFTA Awards, then slipped it in to the show that night. There was no comeback and no complaints.'

In April Dave appeared live on stage at the glamorous dinner and entertainment venue the Talk of the Town in London (now the Hippodrome) for a six-week season to a great reception. Set just off Leicester Square, this was one of the most sophisticated evening venues in London, where diners were entertained after their meal and was highly suited to the late-night adult humour of Dave Allen. He achieved a life-time ambition and appeared on the same stage as Judy Garland.

The 1970s had started quietly and successfully enough, but as always he was split between Australia and the UK and was offered the opportunity to return to make another series of *Tonight with Dave Allen* in Australia. It was a very strategic move as it allowed any fear of overexposure in the UK to disappear and in fact made television executives wait eagerly for his return, as had the Australians. When he returned to Australia, he was about to cause a sensation live on air that would be talked about for years.

On 18 September 1971 a live ninety-minute special of *Dave Allen* went out on Nine Network in Australia. Patrick Condon, the executive producer, remembers, 'Peter Cook and Dudley Moore had been upstairs in the board room [the green room] all evening. The show started at 7 p.m. By the time the floor manager came to collect them, at about 10 p.m., they had both been drinking quite a lot. Peter stood up and said that he needed "to take a piss" and went off. Dudley went downstairs with the floor manager and was shown on to the set.

'Dave welcomed him and asked him where Peter was. Dudley told Dave on air that he was "taking a piss". Dave just said, "Fuck him, then." Well, the audience were laughing at all this, and Peter eventually joined them on the set. Don't forget this was live television.

'There were over three hundred people in the studio audience that night, and one of them asked Dave how often he masticated. It wasn't a "plant", someone who had been put there to ask the question, it was just someone having a laugh, but the double entendre was clear, and Dave replied, "Three to four times a day."

'The interview carried on, and Dave was asking Peter questions, but the problem was that he [Peter] was slurring his replies. Peter Cook was speaking so quickly that no one could understand him. Dave's producer told him to try and get Peter to slow down and they would go to a commercial break. Dave told the producer to go masticate himself.' (It was subsequently reported in the press that the word he used was 'masturbate'.)

'It got worse from then on, and the switchboard went into meltdown,' Warren Seal said. 'John Collins, the producer of that show, got into all sorts of trouble for all of this.'

Patrick Condon continued the story: 'Dave was leaving for England the next day and I got a phone call from Sir Frank

Packer [father of Kerry Packer] the next morning. He told me to fire Dave for using unacceptable language, like "fuck" and "masturbate". I was quite happy to say, "Yes, Sir Frank, of course I would sack him," as I knew Dave was oblivious to all of this and was safely on his way home, up in the air at thirty-five thousand feet drinking champagne. Although he was banned for two years, so were Peter Cook and Dudley Moore. We could have had the ban removed at any point.'

In 1972 Dave Allen appeared in his first straight theatre role in England as Dr Daly in *A Pagan Place* by the Irish writer Edna O'Brien at the Royal Court Theatre on Sloane Square in London. Directed by Ronald Eyre, Dave received good reviews, and it was obvious that he was no longer just a television comic or personality.

Michael Sharvell-Martin said, 'I saw him in *A Pagan Place* and he was superb. I said to Dave that he could do anything now. He was at his peak of popularity. We were both with the same agent, Richard Stone, and I told Dave to just phone him up and tell him that you want to play Hamlet and he would be able to do it anywhere, but that wasn't what he wanted to do. He liked the diversity of interviewing, sketches and his stand-up routine.'

Kerry Jewel, son of Jimmy Jewel, shared the same agent as Dave and also did some writing for him. Kerry remembered, 'Richard Stone, who was both our agents, was affectionately known as "the Colonel". He got the title because he came up through ENSA, which was the division set up during World War Two to entertain the troops. You know, people like Milligan and Sellers and all those people came through there. And the Colonel, when he left the army, set up the Richard

Stone office and handled some of the biggest names in the industry: Benny Hill, Dave Allen, and I think Richard Stone Associates handled them to their death in both those instances. And I was in that office; he handled me as a comedian. I would often meet Dave through that connection, and I worked with him a couple of times as a writer and performer.

'Richard Stone had the unique combination of a lazy eye and a glass eye. It was a difficult set of challenges to deal with when you were talking to him. His eyes would wander so that you never quite knew which one to look into. I never knew which one was false because it was so good.

'One day Dave and I came out of his office, and I turned to Dave and said, "Dave, you've known the Colonel for a long time, which is the glass eye?"

'Dave replied, in a strong Irish brogue, "You know the one with a little bit of warmth? Well, that's the glass one."

'Because the Colonel was a notoriously tough negotiator and producers used to tremble in their boots if they had to get a deal for Dave Allen or whoever else he was handling, they knew it was going to be very tough.' When Richard Stone died, Vivienne Clore for Richard Stone Associates became David's agent.

On BBC2 that year, series two of *Dave Allen at Large* achieved the biggest audience ever for that channel. It was shown fortnightly on Thursdays at 9.20 p.m. While Dave's career was nearing its peak, his brother, Johnny, had gone from Butlins in a totally different direction. Ignoring his natural performing talent, although Dave would later say that his brother never wanted to perform, Johnny O'Mahony had built on his experiences at Butlins, where he had looked after the rigging at Filey and helped on all the shows, and moved to the Aldwych Theatre, the home of the RSC. (Prior to this he had worked in most of the London theatres on Shaftesbury Avenue as a 'showman'.)

Johnny was a popular member of the crew. Caroline Howard remembers him well: 'Johnny was the props master for the big tours in the 1970s for *Coriolanus* and Peter Brook's production of *A Midsummer Night's Dream*. I was an assistant stage manager at the time and relied on Johnny to help me with the running of the shows. He was very supportive and extremely funny.

'We went all over Europe with *A Midsummer Night's Dream*. Alan Howard and the then artistic director Terry Hands really liked him. Of course Alan Howard was Irish so that helped. Johnny was a jack of all trades really; he would help all the departments.

'Johnny never made a thing about Dave being his brother; in fact he didn't tell me for a long time. My dad was a great fan of Dave's, and even when my parents came to Paris to see me on tour and I introduced them to Johnny as one of the guys I was working with, Johnny didn't mention it. They got on really well, as my dad is from Dublin.

'We had a tough time in Paris where we only had a few interpreters, and Johnny had promised me that the local crew had understood everything that he had told them about the scene changes. Of course, when we got to the scene change, the crew had set everything the wrong way round, but Alan Howard didn't mind at all. Everyone liked Johnny. One day he decided that I was being too bossy, so he put me in a wardrobe skip [wicker basket] and locked it.

'He was very good with the actors, the cast, and wouldn't take any nonsense from them. If they came on to the stage making demands, not realising that the crew had been up all night, Johnny would just bark at them, and Alan and Terry really respected him for that. He was well liked by everyone.'

Friend John Jordan used to meet up with Johnny and listen to his stories. 'I used to meet Johnny O'Mahony in the pub Nell of Old Drury,' he remembered. 'I was working at the Royal Opera House at the time.

'All the crews from the London Coliseum, Covent Garden, the Fortune, the Lane [Drury Lane] used to meet up at one of the various pubs around Covent Garden. We used to do a circuit of them all. Johnny used to tell very funny stories and was very well liked. I probably should have listened to the stories more.'

In 1973, when the last of the 1,056,000 tiles was in place, a famous Sydney landmark was finally opened. It was ten years after its original expected completion date of 26 January 1963. Her Majesty Queen Elizabeth II formally opened the Sydney Opera House on 20 October 1973. Dave Allen appeared on a double bill with the British comedian and star of *On the Buses* Reg Varney at the concert hall on Sunday 14 October. Their show was the third in a series called *Sunday Night at the Sydney Opera House* and part of the celebrations for the opening. (Rolf Harris performed at the first on 30 September and Petula Clark starred on 7 October.) ABC also lifted the two-year 'live' television ban on Dave.

John Moulton was his tour manager in Australia in the 1970s. 'Before I met Dave and became his tour manager for a tour of Australia, my wife and myself, together with just about everyone we knew, were fans of his television work both from the UK and in Australia.

'It was Patrick Condon, as director of AGC Paradine, who introduced us and asked me to become Dave's tour manager. From that day forward until the end of the tour my memories are of the best of times and of a man who was wonderful to be around. He had the best comedy timing of anyone that I ever had the privilege to work with.

'The routine was that just before the curtain went up the tumbler – a large one – was firstly filled with ice and then a well-chilled bottle of Moët or another quality champagne was poured over the ice and placed on the table beside his stool. The curtain went up. The performance was as brilliant as always and then at the interval we repeated the process. It might interest you to know that he never had Scotch on the stage when I worked with him.

'Two well-iced glasses of champagne a night to me seemed rather light by my drinking standards, given I had just completed a series of rock-and-roll tours.

'The only other person I have worked with who drank his champagne in this manner was Rudolph Nureyev, but in his case it was post-performance, luckily for his partners. It is still my favourite drink when partaken of in this way, and whenever I do, thoughts of them both are ever present.'

Dave Allen left Australia for England via New Zealand to make his first ever appearance there. In New Zealand his short tour, despite plane strikes which delayed his arrival, was a huge success. The press claimed that this was the Dave Allen that NZBC wouldn't let them see, that he was 'bawdy, cheeky, rude, and he was happily blasphemous'. This was a little unfair to NZBC as Dave's stage show was very different to his television shows. Dave played Auckland, Hamilton, Wellington and Christchurch.

Dave Allen told a reporter from the *New Zealand Listener* in a rare interview about himself that he 'made it in this business by pure accident and then I found I enjoyed it. It has given me great pleasure, and I know how lucky I have been. Sure, I make a reasonably good living.'

He continued with an unusual reference to his early life, 'But there wasn't a lot of pleasure in the past. And that's the main thing now. I walk quietly. I shun publicity. I go my own way. I don't mix in theatrical society, and I have very little interest in the showbiz crap.'

This quiet side of Dave Allen was what appealed to all of the people he worked with, and his circle of friends became wide and very varied. They weren't all television or theatre folk. He maintained contact with the people he had met touring England at the start of his career. He continued, 'I suppose that within my own circle of friends I would be regarded as a funny man. But I don't go out looking for laughs, and I don't walk around telling gags. I should think that most people find me very dull. In fact I'm sure of it. I can often see it in their eyes. They seem disappointed that I seem to play the role of undertaker at most parties. I'm a drinking man. I just like drinking with friends. I use it as a prop on stage as a way of getting to know people. I'm a natural introvert who has to go out there and project part of myself that is outward-going. I couldn't do it unless I was in absolute control.'

And on his home country: 'Don't think I romanticise Ireland. You see, the art of conversation is not dead over there. They savour the language, and they tell a wonderful story about anything – selling a cart, getting drunk and falling on your nose, anything. Not that there's an Irishman telling gags in every pub. But I go into a lot of them and there are many people who can tell a better story than me.'

Tony Goodliffe was a booking agent for Dave's shows at Auckland Town Hall. The shows were so successful that they had to add more shows. 'We started out with just the four shows. Every time I went to the box office the shows were sold out so we added another show. If I remember rightly, we ended up with nine or ten shows just in Auckland.

'Of all the one-man shows, Dave was supreme. No script, no music and no one-liners. He had such a great knack of making everyone feel welcome. He created an intimate atmosphere, so that everyone felt as though they were his guest. He was "out front" in my experience, a great guy. I couldn't believe it when I read about his death in the *Herald*.

Brian Robb, the manager of the Opera House in New Plymouth on North Island, remembered a 'full house' in 1973. 'He was always formally dressed for the shows as we expected in those days; probably we would say it was "stiff and starchy" nowadays. I remember chatting to him about gardening. He sounded as if he really enjoyed gardening.'

His comedy and the show were ever changing and

evolving. It was still completely different to the standard racist or sexist jokes that most of the stand-up comics were doing at the time. Dave explained, 'I don't particularly like racist gags. I don't mind telling gags about Australians or New Zealanders or even blacks or Chinamen as long as it doesn't put them in a position where the listener actually feels superior to the people you are talking about. I don't like that type of thing. What I do is take a situation, perhaps Irish, perhaps English, perhaps a situation involving a drunk, perhaps not. I don't tell drunk gags more than any other, but they do work because you can get many different moods from a man when he's drinking.

'Who knows why a man does or doesn't laugh at a gag? Humour is an immediate thing. A laugh is an immediate, instinctive reaction. You may have your immediate reaction and laugh or not, surely after a moment you can't help thinking of the reality behind the gag.'

At the end of this interview Dave talked to the reporter about plans to make a documentary about second-generation blacks in Britain. After his success with *In the Melting Pot*, it would have been a revealing, insightful piece, had it happened.

In England Dave was back on the BBC with series three of *Dave Allen at Large*. Then in November he accepted a totally different challenge and took on the twin roles of Captain Hook and Mr Darling in the Robert Helpmann production of *Peter Pan* staged at the London Coliseum. Playing opposite him was Maggie Smith. It achieved mixed reviews and comments that it shouldn't have been performed in such a vast theatre. The London Coliseum, designed by Frank

Matcham had a capacity of 2,200 seats, but the stage was over a hundred feet wide. The reviewers would have preferred to have seen it in one of the more intimate theatres.

Despite its mixed reception, Dave enjoyed playing the evil Captain Hook and scaring all the children. Since childhood he had always been fascinated by horror stories. He was renowned for telling horror stories to his children, and Rocky Mason remembers a time when they went to visit one of the Redcoats' managers. It was a winter night and snowing. Dave and Rocky turned up at this Redcoat's house to find that he had a few hours' drinking time in ahead for them. Rocky and Dave sat and drank until their friend fell asleep in his chair. The two of them didn't want to leave; they had had a lot to drink too, and it was a bitterly cold night.

As Rocky Mason explains, 'While Dave and I sat talking, we heard some giggling on the stairs. Dave went out to have a look and found our mate's children sitting on the stairs. They had been listening to us. Dave told them to come in and join us. They sat on the floor in front of him and listened wide-eyed to his ghost tales. This went on for a long time until the wife came hurtling downstairs. She was furious with Dave as she thought he had deliberately woken them up. As she hauled the children back upstairs, she threw us out of the front door and into the snowy night.'

Simone Condon remembers the ghost stories well: 'I was a child of about four or five when I first met Dave. He and my dad, Pat Condon, worked together. When he came to Australia on tour, I only knew him as a funny man who told scary ghost stories.

'My first memories of him were when he used to come to lunch or dinner and gather all the kids together, sit us on the floor, turn out the lights and tell horrific horror stories. They scared the pants off me. My grandmother would make him a cup of tea to keep him going during the stories. He was very particular about his tea and had to have it "just so".'

Michael Condon, Simone's brother, continued, 'I must have been about four or five when Dave told me and my friends these amazing stories and did some magic tricks. Even now whenever we are all together, someone always mentions the magic tricks and those stories. They were so vivid.'

But Dave also wanted to share his passion for fear and scary stories with adults and in 1974 published his book *A Little Night Reading*, a compilation of the most famous horror stories. The signing session for this book was held in one of the most historical pubs in London, Ye Olde Cheshire Cheese. Set off Fleet Street, it had been a meeting house for hundreds of years for wits and journalists. One of the seats has a brass name plaque on the back for Dr Johnson. The book was a great success, and it was yet another side of Dave Allen.

Back in England for a few months, while the BBC showed a retrospective collection called *Dave Allen Once Again*, he was busy researching a series that was a development of his fascination for people who were out of the ordinary. He was back with ITV.

Dave Allen in Search of Great British Eccentrics was the result of 5000 miles of travelling and produced a unique look at the English. In Durham he found a group who guarded the leeks in their gardens each night. They fed the leeks on Guinness and blood. When he was asked if they were 'eccentric', Dave replied, 'Possibly not in Durham, for you can make a fortune growing the biggest leeks.' Dave found a man who thought there was no up or down, that the sun is cold, the Earth is shaped like a split apple, and the moon is a disc covered in 'plasticine phosphorous'. The man told Dave that 'the whole universe is really a silver-coated pill and not very large, about a thousand miles across.'

After meeting and filming them, he came to the conclusion that if anyone was eccentric it 'was me. Eccentrics are not slightly mad; they are slightly sane. They have discovered the ability to step when they choose into another world where they have a lot of fun, where they can live as long as it suits them as part of the most entertaining dream their fertile minds can make up. It is a good thing indeed that England has always kept a special place for its eccentrics.'

The series was a great success. The Dave Allen shows were broadcast and sold around the world, and in Denmark Dave was voted 'Top Foreign Television Star'.

At the end of the year he toured New Zealand for the second time. This time it was a long stay and time to take in all the scenery and do some painting as the tour took him to both islands. Then he returned in the New Year to Australia to tape four fifty-minute episodes of *The Dave Allen Show in Australia* for Seven Network, which ran as shortened episodes for two years. (These starred Dave with Tina Bursill, Gordon Chater, Carla Hoogeveen, Judy Morris, Eric Oldfield, Carol Passmore and Martin Phelan.) He also recorded six ninety-minute shows for Nine Network. The honorary Australian was back in his second country for the first of two visits that year. He was touring on his own again, with Judith at home in England.

Writer Peter Vincent worked on the television series in Australia with Dave. 'It was a great time in Australia with Dave. Austin Steele was the producer. Dave and I used to meet at 9.30 a.m. and start mapping out some scenes. We stopped at 11 a.m. to have Sydney oysters, which were cheap and wonderful. Our working days seemed to be quite short between the oysters and lunches. I remember, though, we suddenly had just one day to do all the ideas for a show, and we felt very smart that we had done it in just one day.

'Dave and I only had one row. He was such a generous man, and he never let me pay for any meals out in Australia. I really had to have an argument with him in the lift one day, as I said that it was about time I paid for a meal, but he would have none of it.

'There was quite a lot of stress with this series. Austin, for one reason or another, kept altering the running time of the shows. Dave was going mad because it would fluctuate five minutes in either direction. I could sympathise with both sides. They had a great row, and in the way that these things get very silly and really quite funny, when we were working, Austin would phone through to us and Dave would answer. Austin would ask Dave to hand the phone to me then said, "Tell Dave that ..." It was just one of those silly things really.

'We also got into some scrapes as well. The series was shot in Melbourne and Sydney. The night we had finished at the Melbourne studios, we had a champagne celebration in one of the rooms. None of us realised how late it was, and of course we were horrified to discover that we had been locked in. Took us hours to get out.

'We eventually made it back to the hotel, which had a swimming pool on the roof. We continued the party up there in the pool, but some of the other guests complained, so Dave and all of us were thrown out, nicely, from the pool. It was a night of adventures.

'Dave was a lovely guy. Whenever we had a spare moment, we would wander round antique shops or just go out and see things. He always wanted to be looking at things. He was a great collector of blue and white china as well. He also made the best salads. I had some great lunches with him in his garden in Kensington. He knew all the names of the butterflies. Dave was always painting something, and we had some very good days out there. I think his paintings were an unnoticed talent.'

At the height of his success there were opportunities all over the world. He appeared in New York in ABC's salute to Lew Grade, starring alongside Julie Andrews, Peter Sellers, Tom Jones and John Lennon. In London he appeared at the Royal Court Theatre for a fund-raising gala in aid of the theatre roof restoration. Then on his way back to Australia and a tour of all the major cities, he appeared in a five-week season in Hong Kong. It would be a challenge to see how he could ever be accused of being 'overexposed' in any country.

In 1975, however, controversy was going to catch up with him in England. One of his favourite subjects for his sketches was about to cause outrage. The sketch showed Dave as the Pope, stripping on the steps leading to a church. Members of the congregation of the town in which it was filmed wrote to the BBC. Two hundred thousand reported complaints from Roman Catholics were received by the BBC, and they boycotted his programmes.

In an interview in New Zealand Dave said, 'Which is not a lot when you take into account twelve to fifteen million viewers.'

A British journalist phoned the press office at the Vatican in Rome to get a response from them about this supposed outrage and was probably surprised that the press officer responded with a phlegmatic, 'We would like to think the Church has a sense of humour.'

Back at his childhood home in Firhouse, his jokes were getting a mixed reception. 'Personally, I didn't like the Pope stuff, when he poked fun at the Pope. You had to recognise a level of respectability, and the Pope is pretty high up,' said Rosemary Delaney. While Mick McKenna said, 'I don't think people were shocked at the content of his humour. We were reasonably rounded in education, and I think most people felt it was a healthy thing that someone was able to take on the Church and poke fun. We felt that it was time that the dominance of the parish priest was opened up to a slagging. I wouldn't have been anti-Catholic per se, but I still felt it was a good thing and it was a good thing for Ireland.'

This mixed response seemed to be widespread north and south, as Sean O'Hagan wrote in the *Observer* in March 2005: 'My father considered Dave Allen a comic genius, my mother thought him a blasphemer.

'In our house in Armagh in the early seventies the weekly show, *Dave Allen at Large*, made for tense viewing even, especially, when it had you in stitches. This dilemma was repeated in Catholic households across the province.

'He was the one person in the world who told Irish jokes that weren't self-denigrating. Yet, he made us squirm all the same when he mocked priests, bishops, archbishops and – "God forgive him" I can hear my mother say – the Pope. The joke as the ultimate act of revenge.'

Dave once said, 'The institution you never laughed at in Irish society as a kid was the Church, whether it be the Catholic Church or the Church of Ireland. It was all right to snigger at the Church of Ireland, but certainly not laugh at the Church of Rome.

'A man goes to heaven, and St Peter shows him around. They go past one room and the man asks, "Who are all those people in there?"

'"They are the Methodists," says St Peter. They pass another room and the man asks the same question. "They are the Anglicans," says St Peter.

'As they are approaching the next room, St Peter says, "Take your shoes off and tiptoe by as quietly as you can."

'"Why? Who is in there?" asks the man.

'"The Catholics," says St Peter, "and they think that they are the only ones up here."'

In 1976 series five of *Dave Allen at Large* was shown on BBC2 in an early slot of 8.15 p.m. By now the Dave Allen shows were an institution around the world and his take on the English language was becoming an obsession – 'If it's sent by ship then it is cargo, but if it sent by road it is a shipment.'

Dave Allen was not going to be deterred from his religious gags, but there were some that were not shown. 'I designed a tableau of the manger in Bethlehem. Dave had scripted it so that the three wise men and Joseph ripped off their robes to reveal dinner jackets,' said designer Richard Morris. 'The top of the crib rotated to reveal a roulette wheel, and the whole set changed into a casino. The studio audience thought it was marvellous. Obviously someone thought that it was too near the mark, and it was never broadcast.'

Richard continued, 'Dave was living by Ham Common, near Richmond in Surrey at the time, and Paddy Russell, the director of *Z Cars*, always used to use Dave's house and drive if we had any filming to do locally. Dave never minded, and his house appeared in lots of episodes. I suppose I was quite in awe of him. He was very famous by the time I came to work with him. Even though I had designed shows like *The Onedin Line*, this was very different doing something so specific for a star.'

The shows were always shot in two halves. Peter Laskie, the assistant floor manager on Dave's shows at the time, explains, 'We were out on location first of all doing the sketches. There was one that we shot on the site of what is now the Millennium Dome. It was a very dark sketch about Dave being the last man alive after the nuclear holocaust. The second part of the shoot was done in the studio with an audience, and, of course, Dave was on his stool.

'I remember telling some friends of mine in the States in the eighties that I was working with Dave and they were very impressed. They had watched all of his shows on a public service channel and thought he was really the best comic of his type. I found him such an easygoing and nice man.

'There was a sketch that went wrong. It achieved internal fame at the BBC in a health and safety video. It showed Dave bursting in on his wife who was in bed with a lover. The lover was played by Michael Sharvell-Martin. Dave shoots the lover in the chest only to discover that he is in the wrong house.

'Although the gun had blanks in it, Michael suffered from powder burns which took days to grow out. He was all right but covered in embedded soot lumps, so it was never shown except on training days showing that it could happen to the best.'

Sabina Franklyn, daughter of actor William Franklyn and one of the regular cast members of the 'specials', enjoyed her life as a 'nun' in the programmes. 'I had been working at what we called "The Hilton Towers", the old North Acton rehearsal studios for the BBC. It was rather like a boarding school, with three rehearsal rooms on each floor and a canteen where we all met up. I had just finished what I called my long-dress period. I had just appeared in the eighties production of *Pride and Prejudice* directed by Cyril Coke. James Moir, who was head of comedy at the time, asked me to audition for Dave Allen. It was great fun because I could let rip and have fun disguised as a nun. Dave spent all his time going in and out of his caravan, making amendments to the script and coming up with new ideas.

'We were just outside Oxford, staying at the Marlborough Arms, near Woodstock. Somehow we were always filming in the depths of winter, but when you are working with someone like Dave, it is a joy because any downtime you have is spent in hysterics, although I always felt that there was a deep, pensive sadness about him. I have worked with a lot of comics – Mike Yarwood and Dave of course – and they all have this pensive, quiet side to them.

'Dave did some marvellous twists on some famous commercials. The Milk Tray ad was one of my favourites. This is the man in black who climbs mountains, drives speedboats and "all because the lady loves Milk Tray".

'In Dave's version there was no punchline to this skit, just a close-up of my rotten teeth from eating too many chocolates. I did another one too, this time based on the Camay soap advertisement that was doing the rounds. They always had a star sitting in front of a huge Hollywood starlet-style dressing table. I played the star and dipped my fingers off camera into a large pot of what the viewers would think was Camay, but instead as I wiped it on my face, the camera pulled back to show a tub of Stork margarine.'

James Moir, the producer of two of the Dave Allen specials, said, 'He had a vivid eye for recreating classic scenes. He did one where he played Judas Iscariot with a shot of an American Express card and of course the line "That will do nicely."'

It wasn't always an easy relationship between this highly creative comic and his broadcasting masters, as James Moir reveals: 'Dave was speechless when the BBC wouldn't show one of the ads that we had done.'

Sabina Franklyn continued, 'The Denim aftershave ad was quite a sensual one. All you saw in the real ad was a woman's hand slowly unbuttoning a guy's denim shirt and his hand would suddenly reach up to stop her.

'Of course in Dave's version my hand slowly unbuttoned the shirt, and then the man grabbed my hand and put it on his crotch. It was very funny; the audience was in hysterics, but the BBC said it went too far. Dave was resigned, in a way, when they told him that they weren't going to show it. It was so silly, though; there were far more obvious things being shown on television on both channels at that time. I think that was when he started to get really disenchanted with the BBC, although I felt his work wasn't so good when he crossed back over to ITV.'

In the downtime from television Dave continued to appear around the UK and starred alongside Johnny Mathis and The Shadows at the Hippodrome Theatre in Coventry in a sell-out concert.

In 1977 RTÉ (Ireland's public service channel), in a slow reaction to the stripping Pope and presumably because of other pressure, banned all programmes by Dave Allen. Sean O'Hagan noted in his obituary of Dave Allen in March 2005 that 'In his homeland his [Dave's] pay-off line – "May your God go with you" – never had a chance to fall on deaf ears.'

In 1978 *An Evening with Dave Allen* toured the UK. This one-man show went across the country. These stage shows were very different from the television format. It was on stage that he developed his observational humour, the rambling tales and rage about everyday objects and his view on day-to-day situations, while on television he perfected the long shaggy-dog tales and sketches.

When it was announced that Dave would be appearing at the Theatre Royal in Norwich, the box office was inundated with calls and the season was a sell-out. The self-styled workaholic had broken all the box-office records for his friend, Dick Condon, the general manager of the theatre. The special of *Dave Allen at Large*, shown on BBC2 in April, was successfully entered for the Montreux Festival and won the show a Silver Rose. He was also nominated for an Emmy. Dave finished the year with a ten-week sell-out season at the Vaudeville Theatre in London. He was getting great reviews and allowed the television fans to see his 'other' show.

Even the BBC was not immune to the air of discontent and was hit by a strike for two days before Christmas. There were blank screens on BBC1 and BBC2 except for a sound-only news bulletin at 10 p.m. each night.

In 1979 the opportunity came for Dave Allen to return to acting. He starred on ITV in *One Fine Day* by Alan Bennett, playing the role of George Phillips. He got good reviews, but the workaholic in him returned him almost immediately to Australia for a ten-week tour.

Pat Condon, who promoted Dave's stage shows in Australia, remembers Dave and him taking the slow way home, the scenic route, one day. 'We were driving back from Hobart, I think. Dave wanted to do some of his drawings or paintings. He was always painting. We stopped somewhere for me to get something for us to eat, and he sat watching some women use an ATM. When I got back to the car, he started to develop this idea about machines that suck in your card, take your identity and get to know everything about you. He was fascinated by the idea that a machine could belch at you and throw the card back out at you with no money.

'Two days later the whole idea appeared in his show. It was incredible to watch him do that and a privilege to see it happen.'

The larrikin in Dave Allen was still present, especially among children. Simone Condon remembered tricks that Dave played on her as a child: 'Dave loved playing tricks on people. One time he took me to a Chinese restaurant when I was about eight and gave me chilli! He roared with laughter when he saw my expression. It was great fun to be with him as a child. He was a larrikin and a prankster.

'I did go to one of his shows when I was older, but his professional life was something vague to me; I was too young to understand how famous he was or indeed his stature. When I got older, he was like a surrogate father to me. He always had time to listen to my problems and help and advise me.'

In August 1979 ITV, which had appeared immune to strike action, was hit by a three-month strike. This strike meant blank screens until October. 1979 was also the year that Margaret Thatcher came into power. Either through luck or planning Dave had managed to be out of England when the television strikes occurred.

When Dave returned to England for his autumn tour, he was to make an historic first professional visit to his home city of Dublin. It was surprising to a lot of people that he hadn't returned to perform before now, and it is unclear as to whether it was sensitivity to his shows' content or lack of theatre availability; presumably it was a fine balance between the two. Until the late 1970s he would have been thought too strong even for a much-warned theatre audience.

On 29 September Pope John Paul II landed in Ireland for the third of his pilgrimages. The Holy Father was on a hectic schedule to four provinces. His first stop was Dublin, where he delivered an open-air sermon to an estimated crowd of 1.5 million, nearly a third of Ireland's population at the time. The entire Dublin police force had all leave cancelled for the duration of the visit. Then he went on to Drogheda, Clonmacnois, Galway, Knock, Maynooth and Limerick. The Pope left for America the day that Dave Allen landed in Dublin.

Allen was invited on to *The Late Late Show*, where Gay Byrne interviewed him and later said that 'He was a very nice guy and very clever.'

An Evening with Dave Allen was part of the Dublin Theatre Festival, and he was appearing at the historic Gaiety Theatre. With the Pope's visit so close to Dave's and RTÉ having banned anything by Dave Allen in 1977, there was some trepidation about this stage show. While the audience loved it, the critics' reviews were mixed, which was not surprising. But if anyone was expecting controversy, they were disappointed. (At the end of the tour he filmed a forty-five-minute special for BBC1, which was broadcast on 28 December.)

The 1970s had seen the coming of age of Dave Allen, proficient on television and stage whether as an actor or on tour with his own shows. He was shrugging off the supposed competition by being himself and therefore still different from all the other comics and entertainers. He was hugely successful but appeared to be always searching for something new to do, something that would stretch his skills even further. With his acute business sense he was able to keep himself just out of reach, by being on either side of the world or busy on unusual projects.

He was always in work, never resting or even, in an actor's sense of the word, unemployed. There was a feeling among his friends that he was being driven by a hunger for work and to be successful but also that there was another reason: a hunger for money, or rather he feared returning to the impoverished situation of his childhood. With his first-hand experience of what having no money was like, he was watching what was happening to his brother, Johnny, who seemed to be struggling not only with alcohol but money as well, very closely.

CHAPTER FIVE

BALLYGOBACKWARDS

'Whenever Dave came to Belfast, we used to go out in my car and head for the country,' said John Jordan, the now-retired technical manager of the Grand Opera House, Belfast. 'He wanted to go where there were no cars, trains, buses or people.

'One day when we were out driving, he asked me if I had heard of a town called Ballygobackwards. I had a feeling that this was going to be a good one and settled back to listen to the tale.

'"It was one of those nice soft Irish mornings, warm with a touch of mist. I was driving along in my car and was trying to get to a small town deep in the countryside of Ireland called Ballygobackwards.

'"I had been driving round in circles for hours, getting more and more lost, when I spotted a man working in a field in the distance.

'"I parked my car, got out and climbed over the flint wall.

I started to make my way over to the man, who was working in the next field.

'"I was halfway over the field when I realised that this wasn't such a good idea as I was sinking up to my knees in a bog. I was now wet and cold.

'"I persevered over the next wall and across to where the guy was working. I called out to him, 'Good morning. I wonder if you could help me. I need to get to Ballygobackwards. Do you know where it is?'

'"He looked up, scratched his chin, thought for a while and said, 'No, I am sorry, I have never heard of it.'

'"I thanked him and resignedly started my trawl back over the wall and across the boggy field. Just as I got to the wall, near my nice warm car, I heard a cry, 'Oy!'

'"I turned round to see the guy waving at me and pointing to another man who must have been working in the same field and gesturing to me to go back to speak to them.

'"I sighed, turned round and squelched my way back over the boggy field, back over the flint walls and back to the field where the men were waiting for me.

'"The man said, 'This is my friend. He hasn't heard of it either.'"

'I nearly drove straight into the Irish Sea when he told me that joke,' remembered John Jordan.

The 1980s saw a change of fortune for Dave Allen. If the seventies were about personal success, the eighties were pivoted around his private life. While his television shows were still hugely successful, the theatre critics in the UK started to compare him to the new generation of stand-ups: Ben Elton, Alexei Sayle and all the others who were coming up the ranks. The new comedians were social commentators and political satirists, hard hitting, fast talking; they were young and very much in vogue. They talked about the money-obsessed, power-dressing, 'lunch-is-for-wimps' yuppies. Dave Allen, with his long tales and observations, wasn't going to compare well under close scrutiny. Nor was he going to be hailed a star in New York on Broadway.

In 1980 Margaret Thatcher had been in power for just one year. Some commentators thought that Dave Allen didn't fare well during the 'Thatcher Years' not as a direct result of her influence but because of the change in style of comics that occurred during her time as Prime Minister.

Following a tour of the UK in 1980 Dave went on another tour to New Zealand and Australia. Then he came home via Hong Kong where he did three performances in 1981. This roaming, whether planned or not, was very clever as it continued to prevent overexposure in any one country. It also allowed for many 'comebacks', although the reality was that usually he had just been 'otherwise engaged' on the other side of the world.

Allen returned to the UK for a season at the Theatre Royal, Haymarket, in London's 'Theatreland' of *An Evening with Dave Allen.* 1981 was a momentous year for the rumoured eighty-Gauloises-a-day comic as he stopped smoking and coined the now-famous phrase 'Why should I pay someone else to kill me?' It is not clear whether this was as a result of a health-scare or whether, as he said to a newspaper but which seems unlikely, he had been standing in duty-free at the airport one day and just decided to stop, there and then.

1981 also saw Dave start work on two series for the BBC. On 20 April BBC1 showed a fifty-minute special, and on Friday 29 May BBC2 broadcast a fifty-five-minute special at 9.30 p.m. These specials starred what writer and comedian Barry Cryer called Dave's 'repertory company'; actors Jacqueline Clarke, Michael Sharvell-Martin, Paul McDowell and Susan Jameson worked on most of the specials (and some of the series) with Dave.

James Moir, a producer at the time remembers, 'I was so very proud to be working with him. I had a lot of affection for him. Peter Whitmore and I cut together *The Best of Dave Allen*, and we were all so pleased with it.

'We had very high production standards, so did Dave, but there wasn't a bottomless pit of money. We did a take on the famous VW ad. We filmed it at an army base in Bicester. Dave had written the scene so knew exactly what was going to happen. The car was dropped from a great height. There were bolts flying out of it, and it landed on the ground right beside him, and he didn't flinch a muscle. He knew we didn't have a second car so he just let it happen.

'Everything he did had verisimilitude. He had such flair with historical scenes. They were always seen through the Irishness of his eyes. We had a scene from *Tom Jones* that was really very graphic. I knew that Jacqueline Clarke felt that it was very near the knuckle. It was all to do with eating a banana and you can probably work out just how lascivious it was. We did show it to a studio audience, but the banana routine wasn't broadcast.

'He did a great tribute to me shot in my office for my fortieth birthday all about the fact that I was probably now just waiting for the pennies to be put on my eyes. He loved all that dark stuff.'

Dave Allen also knew when things should not be broadcast. 'He had written a different angle on "he who casts the first stone" and was playing Jesus,' James Moir continued. 'The idea was that Jesus started throwing pebbles at people at the end of the scene. I am a Catholic and I knew that this was Dave's upbringing. I asked him before we started shooting if he had ever played Jesus Christ. He said that he hadn't but didn't make any further comment. I didn't push him either.

'It was an outdoor shoot with him on the cross and the weather was dreadful. When we looked at it in the edit suite later, he sat there in silence then said, "No, the make-up is ruined by the rain; wig looks bad," and he binned it. I don't know if that was the real reason, and it's not for me to guess, but we didn't show it.'

Barry Cryer, writer and comedian, described himself as 'the new boy' in the writing team of Peter Vincent, Ian Davidson and Dave Allen. 'We would all meet in a room to talk through ideas. Peter and Ian had warned me that Dave used to switch off, slip lower and lower in his seat, until something someone said would spark him off again. The performer rules in a situation like that, and Dave was a perfectionist. The shows come out of discussion, but it was always performer led.

'He had a lot of the demon in him. We were handing over the keys at Twickenham for a minibus for a charity one year. Dave suddenly lunged at me and started snogging me. It was very funny; we ended up on the floor. When I asked him what all that was about, he said that he just wanted to "liven it all up a bit. It stops life being boring." I tried not to get emotionally involved! [Laughing.]

'One evening Dave and I went to the Comic Strip in Soho to see some great comics. The night was hosted by Alexei Sayle, and we watched Jennifer Saunders and Dawn French and an amazing array of talent. I was so impressed by Dave's interest in it all. It was exhilarating.

'The last time I saw him was on the Radio Four quiz *Quote Unquote*, and I was astonished at how he had changed into this wild-haired academic type. Half-moon glasses, tweed jacket, you know, so different from how he started off.

'My wife said to me the first time she saw him, on *Val Doonican* when he was that dapper young man with black hair, that "He had better be funny because I really fancy him."'

The comedian Dickie Henderson had been successful on the career life-or-death stage that is Broadway in New York. He said that it was because he altered his act to become more American. Others Brits hadn't been so successful. Dave Allen knew what had happened to the other comics who had tried to sell themselves to the other side of the Atlantic but thought it was his time. He headed off for a two-week season at the Wilbur Theatre, Boston, as a 'trial' before moving on to New York.

The Boston critics didn't warm to his relaxed style, however. They called him bleak, cold, circular and offensive.

They said that his style was satirical and deadbeat and finally – and inexplicably to most people who had seen his shows in Australia, New Zealand and the UK – that he was on stage for far too long. This sort of review was a body blow to the man who had originally modelled himself on Jerry Lewis. It was an inauspicious start.

Dave headed for the Booth Theatre on Broadway in September 1981. Although people had watched the BBC shows in the US, he wasn't widely known. Again, it wasn't a success. Clive Barnes, the English theatre critic of the *New York Post*, was the only critic to support Allen. The theatre struggled to be filled during the season, and there were comments that he should have played 'off Broadway'.

Dr Oliver Double commented, 'If you read the reviews you can sense that the US critics were against him because in their eyes he was trying to do what their comics had done for years. They were behaving as though they had seen it all before, but he was treading on their patch. They were being typically imperialistic in their dislike of him.'

1981 was not going to get any better for Dave Allen in England either. What none of Dave's friends knew was that in 1980, he had moved out of the family home, Maplecroft, in Henley-on-Thames, and was living in a bachelor pad in Knightsbridge. 'Ironically [...] a flat that we brought together and that I decorated,' Judith Stott told the *Sunday Mirror*. It was a very sad time for everyone, although as friends had commented, it wasn't surprising. Dave had been working overseas or at full-tilt in England for most of their married life. He was always away touring or filming even when he was in England. Judith's career had been put on hold while

Dave's had been a great success. In the same interview Judith told the *Sunday Mirror* that 'Dave felt that money was the answer to everything. I don't know what it is about comedians, but they just don't seem to be able to face real-life problems.'

During their marriage the Allens had moved many times, living in and around London, Surrey, then Devon and Henley. Actor Michael Sharvell-Martin commented that Dave had been very astute and had invested in property 'all over the place'.

'He kept his divorce totally removed from his profession-al life,' remembers Jacqueline Clarke. 'At the end of one of the series he invited us all to his flat. He always celebrated the end of a series or a special with a meal for all the cast. This time it was at his flat in Knightsbridge, opposite Harrods, and of course we noticed that he was by himself and that Judith was nowhere to be seen, but we would never have asked him.'

Separated from Judith, Dave continued to go out on the road and toured in *An Evening with Dave Allen* for a three-week season at the Palace Theatre, Manchester, and at Birmingham Hippodrome for one week. He was a solitary figure, out on the road alone.

Tony Guest remembers, 'I was the stage manager at the Birmingham Hippodrome at the time. Dave was touring by himself with no help. He turned up with two suits, one black and one white. I used to pass him in his dressing room ironing a couple of very dodgy-looking shirts each night.

'We were completely sold out. I "ran the corner" [gave the cues to lighting, sound, etc. at the stage manager's prompt corner] each night, and I will always remember how spell-bound I was to see Dave in action at such close quarters. Each evening he introduced a different theme into the act, sometimes the same material but delivered in a different order.

'He always invited us back to his dressing room after the show every night. He was truly remarkable.'

In 1983 Dave Allen and Judith Stott were divorced at the High Court in London on the grounds that they had lived apart for over the mandatory two years. Reports in the newspapers and from friends tried to convince the world that it had been done with a smile, but it had not been easy. Judith Stott told Wensley Clarkson in the *Sunday Mirror* on 8 February, 'What makes me bitter is that I gave up my career to help David.' Judith commented on her theatrical entrance at the divorce courts dressed in black, 'I think it shook him [Dave] a bit as he hasn't a good sense of humour.'

With Jane and Edward into their teens they had obvious-ly decided that the children would not suffer from this break-up. Patricia Smyllie remembered, 'He was married to her for nineteen years and told me, "I always ask Judith's advice when I plan to do something new. She has to agree; I would never suddenly decide to do something which might affect the family." He still cared about Judith of course.'

In 1983 Judith Stott's house in Richmond was burgled and, in an horrific attack, she was left gagged and trussed by three burglars. Newspaper reports claimed that she wasn't rescued for ten hours. Pat Smyllie remembers, 'When Dave heard about it, he rushed to see if she was all right. He was a very caring man.'

Dave ostensibly carried on with his working life as usual and returned for a two-month tour of New Zealand. The tour manual, compiled by Phil Warren, said that 'You will remember from your last visit that New Zealand has some unusual, indeed strange liquor licensing laws. These are virtually unexplainable to the uninitiated and have been subject to continuous fiddling in endeavours to bring them into the last quarter of the twentieth century!'

It goes on to say, 'It has been alleged that New Zealand has only two seasons and often on the same day; and, since your last visit, New Zealand has introduced, not without some controversy, the thrill of Saturday-morning shopping.'

Performing in twenty towns and cities, this was a welcome return for 'New Zealand's favourite comedian'. Presented by Phil Warren, Dave Allen played a total of thirty-eight performances. Reece Warren remembers his father, Phil, having a great time with Dave whenever he came to New Zealand: 'Whenever Dave came to Auckland City, their lives were spent working of course, but they talked about rugby, and Dave would cook in our kitchen. He always stayed with my dad when he came to New Zealand. But their best meals seemed to be eating at the side of the road in Invercargill at a pie cart. He was very down-to-earth.

'I have a particular memory of Dave and my dad watching rugby; I thought that the two men were far more entertaining than the match. They were yelling and shouting at the TV.

'One time they bet on the match; Dad on the Australian team, and Dave on the All Blacks [NZ]. Dave won and gave me the winnings. My father really didn't approve of that. I thought it was great!

'Dave was pro-NZ and was very interested in NZ wine; I remember that. Dave enjoyed champagne after his show. My dad once sent him a case of L&P [a NZ soft drink] for one Christmas as a joke. They always kept in touch by letter, especially when Dave wasn't doing a tour to NZ.

'My parents didn't always have dinner with the entertainers that dad (Phil) promoted, but they had a special relationship with Dave. I really think that Dave was the first person to develop situation comedy rather than stand-up.'

Reece was surprised not only by Dave's untimely death but also by the small (and belated – nothing was said for days after his death) mention it got in the New Zealand media, 'given the number of times Dave had performed to packed houses here'.

In Wellington he played the St James Theatre, Courtney Place, and on 19 October Dave got a close-up of the workings of Parliament with the Hon. Russell Marshall, CNZM. 'In the early 1980s I was in my fourth term as a Labour MP in the NZ Parliament, the third in succession in opposition,' recalled the Hon. Russell Marshall. 'Distractions from the frustrations and the tedium were welcome. I gradually realised that as an MP, it was possible to meet, even to host, interesting personalities from the rest of the world. For example Billy Connolly entertained my family once at lunch in our parliamentary dining room. Phil Warren, an Auckland City local body politician and entrepreneur, facilitated a number of these arrangements. One time Phil and I had arranged that I would host a meal for Harry Secombe, but sadly Harry had a serious health problem early in his New Zealand tour and left for home before we were able to meet.

'Feeling that he owed me, Phil asked if I would like to meet Dave Allen and even to have lunch with him. I jumped at the opportunity. Dave was well known to Kiwi TV viewers, perched on a stool, part of a digit missing, with his delightful, dry monologues. We all liked the way he would take the mickey out of the Irish. As I was later to find with Connolly, Dave Allen was much the same person in real life.

'I remember that I took Dave after lunch to sit on the floor of the House. In those days of a smaller Parliament, there was room for a small number of guests of MPs to sit behind the members in the debating chamber. He must have stayed for some time because I remember him still being there after Question Time when there was a debate on abortion law. I have often since then reflected on how strange, yet also how familiar, it must have been for him to sit in on a debate with so many of the views he might well have heard at Westminster or in the Dail [the Irish Parliament].

'When I was at the High Commission in London, I kept thinking about getting in touch with Dave. We were much of an age, and I deeply regret never making the effort to meet him again.'

Margaret Aitken went to see the show in Wellington. 'He was so handsome and smartly dressed. The show was wonderful. I remember that he spotted a woman in the audience dressed all in white and called out to her, "You're very pure-looking … are you? Are you?" Of course all the audience were laughing at this. He was a great flirt. The theatre was absolutely packed with people of all ages. He had such a wonderful reputation.

'After the show Dave came out into the foyer to meet some of the audience. I was sure he was hitting on me as he suggested that I look him up the next time I was in London. You know he really seemed genuine, and I was tempted. But really I think it was because he was from Donegal and I am from Leitrim and the two counties "touch each other" and we must have been the same sort of age. I run an access radio programme called Capital Irish where we promote Irish entertainers and events. I was so upset when I saw an item on the TV news. They showed one of his great skits where he took bets in the confessional. He will be sorely missed.'

Far away from his personal troubles at home, his reviews in New Zealand were very welcoming. The *Churchill Press*, on 8 October 1983, said, 'Relaxed, congenial and wickedly hilarious, no one can doubt that Dave Allen has done it before. His smooth and suave delivery is totally absorbing, and the content is never predictable.

'The first half of the show briefly examined attitudes to drink, the Irish and launched into the main theme of language – the use of words in contradictory ways. Australian vowels received a hammering with a prime example of "Emma Chisit?" which roughly translated meant, "How much is it?" The American use of language came under scrutiny too.

'His treatment of plane crashes became so convincing

that even as you laughed about the absurdity of the safety precautions, memories of the Korean airline's tragedy arose. The injection of this edge to his humour continued with an extended sequence on nuclear proliferation. While profoundly funny, there was an underlying note of intensity that made the evening more than just a romp through the zany. Mr Allen is the master craftsman of the comic art.'

At the end of his extensive tour of New Zealand, which included such unlikely places as Twizel where he visited over the New Year period, a local reporter noted, 'Had he not been in this small South Island centre, he would have been giving a royal-command performance in London. He'd declined the grand show in the UK in favour of a tour of New Zealand.' [Some of his Irish shots at royalty may have explained his preference.]

He returned to the UK in 1985 and went back to work with his 'repertory company'.

'He used to use my "digs" in London, and I stayed with him nearly two years at his flat in Knightsbridge,' said Michael Sharvell-Martin. 'I learnt everything I know about red wine from Dave – the number of nights we crawled on our knees out of the sitting room along to our bedrooms! But I learnt that with great red wine you don't suffer a hangover.

'We had the same agent at the time, Richard Stone. Obviously Richard was well aware that Dave really wasn't a morning person, and he used to turn up at the flat to see both of us bleary-eyed. Richard probably didn't always see the funny side of it.

'When Dave moved to the house off Kensington High

Street, I used to stay there as well. He was like my brother. I spent most of my time answering the phone, fending off a more and more distraught Judith. This was a long time after the divorce; it was all over, and Dave had had enough of her calls. It was so sad.'

All the cast who worked with Dave faced the same problem as everyone with his unfailing generosity. 'One day I missed an "end-of-term" meal at the Hyde Park Hotel after filming a special or the end of a series,' said Jacqueline Clarke. 'Dave took one of the wardrobe girls over to Harrods to buy me a present because I couldn't make the meal, and I still have this lovely scarf that he got me. He was really very generous.

'In return we all decided one day to get him a present. This was a difficult decision, and it took us hours to come up with this. We got him a silver finger; we called it a "a joint present", and it said on the inscription, "A small gesture from all of us." You can imagine that we thought we had been so clever and funny, coming up with this idea, but Dave had the last laugh as he never ever mentioned it. That was his humour.'

Michael Sharvell-Martin continued, 'It probably ended up as a doorstop in the house. I laughed one day when I noticed that one of his precious awards was keeping his office door open. That was just the way he was. Need something to keep the door open, find something that will do it.'

The 1980s had already seen troubled times for Dave, but they were about to reach a nadir, and it started when Mary

Whitehouse, a campaigner for years on the quality and standards of television and founder of the Clean Up Television campaign, complained about Dave's use of bad language and his attacks on the Church. Then in 1985 Edward, his son, was expelled from Radlett College for smoking cannabis and then was stopped by police while driving through Kensington one night. The police detained Edward and his friend, Jimmy Tarbuck junior, on suspicion of possessing cannabis. They were released on bail. Patrick Condon remembered that 'Dave laughed, of course, but you know he just carried on. Both Jane and Edward spent a lot of time with Dave, even after the divorce.'

Dave was also having a difficult time with his brother, Johnny. They had always been close as brothers, and Dave had watched out for him. But his mother and everyone knew that Johnny had a serious drink problem. For the talented Dave Allen, it was desperately hard to see his equally talented brother, the man who had introduced him to the business of entertaining, just appear to drink his money, his talent and his life away. Dave also knew that Johnny was having serious psychological problems and spent much of his time taking Johnny to see specialists to try to help him.

Johnny had spent the out-of-seasons from Butlins working at London theatres, and John Ramsey remembers him turning up at the stage door of the Globe Theatre on Shaftesbury Avenue (now the Gielgud) many times: 'I always found him a showman's job [working as crew only in the evenings], but he was always really scruffy. My abiding memory of him was that he drank gin and tonic all day long.'

Caroline Howard, who worked with Johnny at the RSC, said, 'In all the time I worked with Johnny, I never saw him eat anything. Drinking was his life, but he was never drunk; he just loved drinking. We were on tour in Munich and we were all having breakfast in this rather snooty hotel and Johnny ordered two steins of beer for breakfast, no food. He was shouting to me over the room to join him because "The beer is so good."

'All the crew at the Aldwych were devastated when one day Johnny O'Mahony just walked out of the stage door. They never saw him again.'

Rocky Mason said, 'There was a story going round that Dave had been sitting at a table in the window of a restaurant with a television producer when a tramp appeared at the window. This guy's face was nearly covered in a black beard, wearing a raincoat with a bit of rope for a belt, and he must have weighed eighteen stone. He looked like a very sad character and he started to bang on the window to catch Dave's attention. When the producer said that they ought to move, Dave said, "Don't be silly that's my brother, Johnny."

'A friend told me that Johnny was working at Wyndham's Theatre at the time as a stage hand, and I thought I ought to go and see him, but they said that I shouldn't as it would upset Johnny and it would upset me. The next time I heard about him was when I read about his sad death.'

When Johnny O'Mahony died, he was homeless, jobless and living at St Mungo's hostel in Earls Court, West London. On 14 January 1986, in what the coroner described as an open verdict, Johnny, aged just fifty-two, fell out of a fourth-floor window of the hostel and died from his injuries.

Dave Allen told the court that his brother had been receiving psychiatric treatment, but he did not know that he had cancer. He had been told that his brother had advanced cirrhosis of the liver and duodenal cancer.

Pat Smyllie remembers, 'One day I was having lunch with Dave and refused a drink. This was when he was appearing on stage at the Royal Court. I was interviewing him for a national newspaper. He looked amazed when I refused the drink. I explained to Dave, "I'm terrified of getting the Irish disease which my family suffer from in a big way. Do you know my family's fortune has literally gone down the loo?" I went on to tell him the story about Smyllie, my uncle. "I was so embarrassed when I heard the pubs around the *Irish Times* had two minutes' silence when my uncle died." While in retrospect it's funny, it is really quite terrifying. Dave didn't say anything so I asked him, "Why are the Irish so obsessed by drink?"

'Dave didn't immediately reply then said, "The Irish can command anything given a few drinks to help them. Although I look a drunk on stage, I certainly am not one off stage. I have also learned the hard way."'

The two remaining O'Mahony brothers, Peter and Dave, were devastated at Johnny's death. 'The RSC crew who went to the funeral were so sad, and they said that Dave had been absolutely distraught,' said Caroline Howard. Dave described the death of Johnny as 'a waste'.

With the death of his brother, his divorce and his own deteriorating health, the 1980s were becoming an increasingly troubled time for Dave. On stage, things were not much better. In October Dave Allen appeared at the Albery Theatre. The Albery Theatre is linked to Wyndhams by a shared stage door, the closeness to the theatre where Johnny had worked cannot have been easy for Dave. His reviews were not good for this season or for the short spell he did at the Arts Theatre Club, a tiny venue for him compared to what he was used to.

Martin Cropper said of *Dave Allen Live at the Arts*, in *The Times* on 31 October 1986, 'Dave Allen is the laziest stand-up comic I have ever seen. The basic problem with Mr Allen's current performance is that he proceeds as though these alternative acts [Alexei Sayle, Rik Mayall, Nigel Planer et al] had never existed.

'Twenty years older (light years behind), Mr Allen can do little but indulge himself in the licence of uttering the "shits" and "fuckings" on which television still frowns.

'From his first entrance, dressed in a very bad suit with double vents like some parodic business colleague on an InterCity train, the Val Doonican of comedy massages his audience's expectations with a parade of feeble material ... in other words the tedious tribulations of a minor mind let loose in the seventies.'

While some critics thought him old-fashioned or trying too hard to compete with the next generation of comics, friends knew that he was 'just being Dave, doing what he wanted to do. He really didn't care at all about reviews or the competition. He knew he could fill theatres around the world and command viewing figures in the millions.'

In complete contrast the *Daily Mail* theatre critic Jack

Tinker said, 'Dave Allen is more of a walking culture shock than a stand-up comedian. He is the most potent thinking man's comedian possibly that these islands have produced. Over two hours of mind-blasting comedy.'

His television appearances continued, first with a special on 31 December 1986 for BBC1 and then as an unexpected guest on RTÉ, ten years after the ban had been in place on any of the *Dave Allen Shows*, in March 1987 when he appeared as the guest of the Church of Ireland Bishop Walton Empey on *Saturday View*. His appearance went without incident or complaint.

His personal life had reached a turning point. He met Karin Stark, who was 25 years old and working for a firm of theatrical producers at the time. They were to be together until his death. Tall and slim, with a dry sense of humour and her own career, she arrived at the perfect moment for a battle-scarred Dave Allen. Their relationship would flourish for the next seventeen years.

CHAPTER SIX

CHRISTMAS IN DONEGAL

In September 1988, the year I met and started working with Dave, the tour of *An Evening with Dave Allen* left Manchester and we started on the real tour. It was an adventure that would introduce us to stalkers and ghosts and which would see us visit many places that held memories for Dave Allen.

On our many Chinese meals around the country we were joined by friends from his club days, croupiers, singers and ladies with no particular job description who all, rather bizarrely, ran dry-cleaning shops; even by 1988 they were all of a certain age. Immaculately dressed, they sat shyly listening to Dave at these meals.

I was still getting used to the quiet, almost dour Dave Allen when he was off-duty and, like everyone before and after me, battling to pay for meals on a nightly basis. I knew that he kept a very close watch on all the costs on tour, yet he seemed almost to want to show everyone that he could pay, that he had money.

Dave Allen had the ability to attract interesting people. We were occasionally joined by some 'noise boys', a team of sound engineers led by Ian Hall. This only happened when we were playing venues that did not have a sound system. Ian was a larger-than-life Scot who had been an oil-rig diver until he had hurt his back and had become a rock-and-roll sound engineer. His humour and his stories kept Dave and I entertained for hours.

In Bradford, at the Alhambra Theatre, Dave became Humpty Dumpty and I became Cinderella. The theatre had called all the dressing rooms after pantomime characters in an attempt to stop the usual conundrum of who gets the 'number-one' or 'star' dressing room.

Dave spent the week phoning everyone at the theatre or me and saying, 'It's Humpty here.' As I pointed out after a week of this, it had been a choice between Humpty or Mother Goose, and I didn't think that any of us could have coped with him calling himself Mother Goose all week. He agreed.

Dave's tour was broken up by welcome visits by his girlfriend, Karin Stark. Her arrival was always welcome, and it made Dave smile and the spark come back into his eyes.

One of the major cities that we visited was Belfast, and I was nervous about visiting this lovely city. Whenever a theatre, ballet or any entertainers toured to Belfast, they stayed at the Europa Hotel, and every week we seemed to be reading stories about the Europa Hotel being bombed. My partner had told me not to be so silly: 'After all, what on earth could happen to you with Dave Allen?' Dave had asked to stay outside Belfast, and we were in a beautiful rural setting so I needn't have worried.

Dave Allen had his own unique view of the troubles: 'What's the fastest game in the world? Well, it's played in Belfast pubs and it's called pass the parcel.'

John Jordan was the technical manager at the Grand Opera House in Belfast, and he had first met Dave in 1984. 'Of course, like everyone, I had been a fan for years. It only took a couple of days of working with this laidback, gentle man before we were like old friends, out everyday driving round the countryside.

'I always used to do the driving and he sat and talked. He used to talk about the early part of his career and how tough it had been for him. We never bothered with any sort of preparations for lunch; we just used to pull up at a local chippy and buy some chips.

'We stopped at Waterfront, a small village, and piled out of the car to go and buy some chips. The girl behind the counter just stared at the sight of Dave Allen coming into that tiny shop and buying chips. What must have been the girl's mother came over to me and said, "Is that the man himself?" I told her that it was all right, but he really could speak for himself and she should ask him herself. It was bizarre that she wouldn't speak directly to him.

'Michael Barnes was the general manager of the Grand Opera House. He had been instrumental in starting the Belfast Arts Festival. He was determined to get this going and keep it running, regardless of the trouble.

'One night he came out to a meal with Marianne, my wife, and Dave. We were going for a curry somewhere along the Lisburn Road. It was a good night and Dave had wound Michael up quite a lot. It ended with Michael standing on a table singing, "I am only a bird in a gilded cage," while Dave just sat looking at him.'

The week we spent in Belfast was spent commuting from our hotel out in the leafy suburb of Hollywood. The downside of staying at the Culloden Hotel, Craigavad, was that the commute to the theatre each evening became a challenge with roadblocks that moved every day and the subsequent re-routing of traffic. We caused a sensation by stopping soldiers to ask the way every night. Every time we stopped Dave would spend twenty minutes being charming to the ad hoc fan club that surrounded us as they saw who it was. It never mattered who approached Dave; he would always talk to them. One man was berating Dave, 'It's all right for you, you don't have to work. You with all your money – wish I had a job like that.' Dave stopped to talk to him and asked him about his job, his life and spent a long time with him. In the end the guy left smiling, and Dave raised his eyebrows muttering, 'Prat.'

Once we had extricated ourselves from the fans and the roadblocks, we would seek refuge in the car park at the back of the theatre, which was surrounded by high-security fencing and CCTV.

One evening, after yet another fraught journey that should have only taken twenty minutes but took twice as long, as I swang right and up into the car park, I rather unceremoniously ran over the foot of a policeman who had stopped to let us through. No amount of body armour or guns could protect him from that. He laughed, though, when he saw Dave Allen. Luckily, I didn't hear any of their comments about my driving. The people of Belfast couldn't have made us more welcome.

In Belfast, Dave updated his routine from the moment he walked on to the stage. He started with a pithy remark about the audience's applause and the fact that it was 'Okay, thank you, but I think you all still have the right to remain silent, don't you?' This was in response to some changes to the law in Northern Ireland regarding the questioning of suspects. The whole audience erupted with cheering.

Anne Muldoon, who was working on the lighting board for the show, remembered, 'I got goose bumps up my arms when he came on stage and said about the right to remain silent. He was unflinching, unafraid.'

Dave had said about Ireland in the 1970s, 'The situation bloody well exists and I'd look stupid if I pretended it didn't. So I use barbed gags to ridicule the people and attitudes I dislike. I feel that way about Bernadette Devlin, and I have no more time for Ian Paisley.

'You see, I think that they are dangerous people, and if I can make them funny or unrealistic to an audience, then I am convinced I am doing the right thing.'

John Jordan remembered a group at the theatre during that week in Belfast in 1988: 'One night Dave had started on one of his ten-minute rants about dogs, dog owners calling for their lost dogs, dogs licking each others anuses then licking their owners' faces and, his favourite, dog shit. I went out into the auditorium to "smell" the audience, you know, to see what was going on and how they were responding. I spotted a whole group sitting on the front row of the dress circle. It turned out that it was a party of husbands and wives from the Bangor Rotarians. They didn't look that comfortable; there was an air of tension about them. I decided to go and speak to Dave in the interval about them.

'Well, Dave just looked at me and said, "That's a pity."

'The show went on and he didn't change anything. I looked out again and, surrounded by all these people having such a good time, they finally started to join in the laughter. He knew that would happen, though. It was very clever psychology.

'One of my favourite routines was about the infamous ten-minute-warning leaflet that the government issued in the eighties. It was about what to do in the event of a nuclear explosion.

'Dave told me that he had gone to his library in Kensington to get hold of a copy of the leaflet, and the librarian had refused to give him it. She told him that he would only use it to "make fun of it".

'Dave told her, "Yes, that's right, that's what I do." She refused point-blank.

'It took him days to get hold of a copy of this, which of course then ended up as the most wonderful, rambling tale of disbelief.

'If you remember, you were told that when you heard the ten-minute warning, you should whitewash your windows to protect against the glare of the blast, unscrew and remove all doors from their hinges and lean them up against walls, in order that you can use them as a makeshift shelter, and all in ten minutes.

'Dave's routine went all through this and the recommendations; he did it very seriously. The audience were half-laughing in anticipation of whatever was coming.

'At the end of the list of things to do in ten minutes he paused, looked at the audience and said, "Now, I don't know about your house, but in mine it would take ten minutes just to find a screwdriver." He was so clever.'

John Jordan remembered another story of Dave's time in Belfast: 'Dave had asked me to get him bags of peat, and of course there was some potcheen. He had asked me to get the bags of peat for him as he couldn't get it in London and he liked a peat fire. I was laughing at this vision of Dave Allen sitting in his house off Kensington High Street, drinking potcheen and burning peat in the fire. He said that he would pretend it was Christmas in Donegal.'

At the end of our season Dave held the traditional champagne party for the crew in his room. Anne Muldoon remembers, 'I waited every night for the "telling-the-time" routine. It was just marvellous. Then of course the party in his dressing room was just so special. No one had ever done that before. I have such warm memories of the time.'

John Jordan continued, 'The Grand Opera House was blown up twice: once just after Dave had been there; the second one nearly demolished the whole place. But it was rebuilt and is back in all its glory as a Frank Matcham-designed theatre.'

Every day in Belfast people presented Dave with bottles of potcheen. I knew that this was illegal hooch. All those bottles of potcheen ended up in one of Dave's bags, which were put in the back of the car, something which I completely forgot about when I was stopped by a customs officer for the ferry back to Liverpool.

She looked friendly and, luckily for me, by the time I had mentioned the magic words 'Dave Allen' and showed her one of the programmes, she didn't seem interested in the contents of the car. It was only when I handed Dave one of his bags at the next venue in Southampton and the bottles chinked loudly that I realised how much inadvertent smuggling I had done. Dave just laughed when I told him about the lucky escape I'd had with the customs officer.

Southampton brought another good week and the surprise of a stalker into our quiet touring lives. She arrived after the show one night, 'disguised' as a journalist. Dave met her in his dressing room, and even when she revealed that she was a fan, he wasn't phased and offered her a drink. She was rather plain looking, late thirties, with short, dark hair. She was quite shy, with nothing out of the ordinary about her at all. At that time in the late eighties we hadn't heard very much about stalkers, so we wouldn't have been looking out for any of the warning signs; we wouldn't have known what we should be looking for anyway.

Neither of us thought much about her until she turned up again in Norwich. Dave was very fond of the Theatre Royal,

DAVE ALLEN: THE BIOGRAPHY

Norwich. He had broken box-office records for the theatre in the past and was friends with Dick Condon, who was the manager. The fact that this woman turned up again wasn't really unusual. All theatre companies and their stars have followers, and sometimes whole families will follow a company around and hover at the stage door to get autographs and take photos of everyone involved in the show. What is always puzzling is how they can afford to do this, especially when there are four of five of them in the family. She asked at the stage door if she could see Dave, and I went to check with him. Dave decided to go out to see her rather than see her in his dressing room, and he did just this as we were leaving the theatre. She talked to Dave for a while, and again nothing really happened.

That night, for a change from the Chinese restaurant we had eaten at for most of the week, we drove round the town and found a very basic restaurant, really just a takeaway with Formica tables and screwed-down chairs. We had a good meal with people collecting takeaways with hardly a second glance at Dave until a couple sat down at the table beside us.

After much nudging, looking, muttering and giggling, they finally plucked up the courage to come over and say, 'You're Bernard Manning, aren't you?' to an astonished Dave. I intervened before a goggle-eyed Dave could say anything, 'No, this is Dave Allen.' The guy calmly told me that I was 'wrong' and 'it' was Bernard Manning. We left hurriedly before vocal blows were exchanged, but Dave was actually rather shocked by this, and I thought that he really looked quite hurt by this case of mistaken identity.

Our next stop was a week-long stay in Plymouth. The hotel car park was in the basement. One morning I was astonished to find our 'fan', our stalker, looking at my car. She was walking all around it and peering into the back. I asked her what she was doing there and she ran. I wondered whether she knew that Dave had his car there as well and whether she had looked at it, but I didn't think so. She had obviously seen me take Dave back and forth in my car and the contents weren't disguised.

I used to spend my daytime off-duty hours driving into Cornwall to Polperro for lunch and to take in the sea air and then back across the beautiful countryside, and I knew Dave liked to see his friends and neighbours in Devon. Dave was going to see his friends that day so I was concerned to let Dave know before he set out. Dave was very phlegmatic about his stalker. He impressed me that he still thought her 'rather sad'. We made an unspoken decision to always park near each other if Dave had driven down to a venue from London. We also watched each other get into our cars, and there was a ceremonial flashing of headlights as we separated, Dave to London and me to the next venue and safely on our way.

Dave started to receive letters that were from this sad woman. He called me into his dressing room one evening to look at these weird, disturbing missives. She said that she would pray for him and described watching him from one of the boxes and kneeling saying her rosary so that he could be helped.

Then, over the weeks the letters took a rather disturbing turn and she started to refer to her uncle who was beating

her because of her infatuation with Dave. I had no experience of anything like this, and we both just stood looking at
these letters. And of course while all this was going on,
Dave had to wipe this from his mind and go on and entertain the thousands who came to see him. We didn't hear
from the stalker again, she just disappeared and the letters
stopped.

Our next stop was Oxford. I didn't know when we visited
this beautiful city that this was where Dave had toured with
the Beatles and had been discovered by the agent who would
take him to Australia. We were playing the very same theatre, the Apollo Theatre (which used to be the Oxford New)
and were staying at the Randolph Hotel, an old, established
hotel featured in *Inspector Morse.*

In the calm and elegance of Oxford we were finally able
to settle into our touring life and were relieved that we
had apparently left our stalker behind. Our routine was
interrupted by meetings with John Thaw, who was
filming *Inspector Morse.* He too was staying at the
Randolph. Dave asked me if I thought he should invite
John to the show. He didn't want to presume that John
would be interested as they didn't know each other well at
all. 'Morse' did come to the show on the first night and,
much to Dave's delight, came round to see him at the end of
the evening.

I continued to be impressed by how caring Dave was. We
had both walked in on each other during awkward telephone calls home and Dave had always asked me whether I
was all right. I had taken phone calls from home for him
during the show about baths overflowing, water damage and

huge confessions as to how it had happened and the general day-to-day messages from people miles away. After the receiver was put down, we had both stood and been each other's sounding board for various outrages caused by BT, Barclaycard, friends, work and the stress that trying to deal with it all long-distance caused.

On our last night in Oxford Dave had a visit from a friend of the family. He arrived on the arm of the stage door keeper, who didn't really know what to do with him. He was falling-over drunk. Dave placed him in a chair and asked me to stay, which I did, while he tried to get a coherent word out of this man. I was keeping an eye on the time as we were getting close to the start of the show. Dave just stood watching this man, with his hands in his pockets, and he looked very sad. I didn't know or remember at the time that this was only a couple of years after Johnny had died. The memories of Johnny and his father's drinking would have been very fresh in his mind.

His friend continued to mumble incoherently and had moved from the 'loving everyone' stage to apologetic and kept saying 'sorry' to Dave. To stop this torture Dave suggested that I could get a taxi for his friend and that he should be on his way. We staggered up the steps of the dressing room and along the corridor with the man between us and finally got him through the stage door and into a passing cab. The stage door keeper looked on in astonishment at the bizarre sight of Dave and I 'man-handling' this drunken man out of the theatre.

When we returned to his dressing room, Dave turned to me and apologised for his friend. It was completely unnecessary.

My partner at the time was an alcoholic, and although I was used to this sort of scene, I think that I was über-sensitive to anyone who was drunk. I accepted the amount that Dave drank on stage, which was really very little – one Scotch and one glass of champagne – as just part of the 'biz', his routine. Later I blamed the tour with Dave Allen for helping me to put on two stones thanks to late-night Chinese meals and the booze that accompanied the meals, which was impossible to refuse. Unlike Dave, though, I didn't have a passion for saunas, and I am not good at swimming in the winter in England.

Dave was always disappointed when he arrived in a favourite touring city or town and discovered that the hotel he remembered was long gone. Apart from his usual room-changing and mine as well – as for some reason hotels decided that we both would be awarded the honour of the room next door to the service lift, the emergency exit or the quadruple bank of lifts – within minutes of checking in we would meet up in reception with a list of problems with both of our rooms. We once discovered that we were in a hotel that was much favoured by the 'by-the-hour' clientele and beat our all-time record by checking out in ten minutes.

I remember on one night in Cardiff we had stayed up in the bar of the hotel quite late. Dave had made a point of speaking to the bar pianist who had the thankless task of playing away in the background to no thanks or applause. Dave bought him a drink and invited him to join us. Dave was genuinely interested in him, his career, where he was playing and shared touring stories with him. We all left for our rooms very late. This was not unusual: Dave went into any conversation expecting to be friends with the other person; it was so interesting. Of course, he had the 'in' as everyone knew who he was and he was unlikely to be rejected, but it was unlike most stars, who are acutely aware of their celebrity and create a chasm between themselves and anyone who might approach them. With Dave, he was just interested to know the person, who they were, what they did, and there was always the possibility that something from the conversation would provide him with a nugget of an idea. If he ever made a mistake with someone, he just walked away with a smile and they were none the wiser.

He also never assumed that another 'star' would want to speak to him. One instance comes to mind when we were in a great fish restaurant in Plymouth with Dave's son, Edward, and some friends of his from university, celebrating Edward's twentieth birthday, when Dave spotted the TV chef Keith Floyd who was sitting at another table. Dave had just finished a long, rambling piece of taradiddle about the loss of his finger in response to Ed's plea to know what had actually happened. Needless to say, Ed didn't get to hear the truth. Dave whispered to me to ask if I thought he should go and say hello to Keith. Apparently he didn't know him. We talked about it, and I said that perhaps Keith was having a private meal. I couldn't see who he was with, and Dave agreed and left it at that. In hindsight I would have loved to have heard the conversation between two such larger-than-life characters.

One night I had been in my room in Cardiff for some time when my phone rang. It was Dave and he was locked in the swimming-pool area of the hotel. Somehow he had found a new route to his room, which avoided the 'lethal' lifts, and had wanted to use the sauna but had gone through the one-way doors only to find that there was no way out. It took me some time to persuade a night porter to come and help me rescue a bemused Dave Allen. He changed rooms after that experience.

Dave used to joke with me that I should write a touring guide to good hotels or places to stay and where the nearest Chinese restaurant was. I didn't of course. I didn't think that there would be many 'Dave Allens' out on the road, but he was convinced that there was a market for it. I told him that I should write the definitive guide to where to buy J&B and champagne around the backstreets of the UK. I had done this so many times for Dave that there must have been a trail of bemused 'offies' all around the UK where I had negotiated the release of their one and only bottle of champagne, regardless of brand on some nights, before baffling them with a request for J&B. On the very odd occasion when J&B could not be found it was a very disgruntled comedian that went on stage. I never found out why he had this passion for J&B. If only we had had the internet back then, it would have been so much easier to find it and get it delivered to each venue. But I learned a lot about champagne on tour with Dave Allen.

One of our touring games was to keep a list of all the whacky names that people had invented for shops. Dave said it was for a friend, but I assumed he was waiting for one to be good enough to make its way into the show. We gathered all the Curl Up and Dyes, the Head Gardeners, the

Whichcrafts and then the Curry Gardens and Curry Cottages that could be found around the UK. They probably ended up in his shows in Australia or New Zealand about the weird British and their signs.

On one occasion in Cardiff we took a wrong turn on the way to St David's Hall and we sat looking for a clue or sign in this backstreet; we could see St David's but couldn't get to it. It was dusk and it was very frustrating. The car behind us decided that we were idiots and foolishly honked his horn at us. I laughed when he honked. Dave Allen looked at me; he was incandescent and said, 'Wait here. I need to speak to that moron.'

I watched in the rear-view mirror as the icon and founder of alternative comedy, grey hair flowing in the breeze, elbows defiantly protruding through the holes of his jumper, hands in pockets, casually walked towards the unsuspecting driver.

The driver wound down his window at the innocently smiling face of Dave Allen. The other occupants of the car looked on in stunned silence. I could see that the driver was trying to work out exactly who this was ranting at him through his window. He knew he knew the face, but the name ...

Dave walked back to our car and got into the passenger side. I could see that the other driver was still sitting in stunned silence. I asked Dave what he had said to the man. 'I just asked him if he knew London at all and whether he knew his way around Kensington High Street. He said that he didn't, so I told him that I would welcome the opportunity to behave like a fucking arsehole when I meet him and honk impatiently at him when he is unfortunate enough to be lost on my home patch.'

Then he said, 'Try left.'

We drove off.

That night, in the show, Dave added quite a lot of vitriol to his routine of drivers and the 'fat bastards' who occupied the road while he was driving.

He continued by complaining about the problems with English signs and pointed to the exit signs in the auditorium. 'Please explain to me why the English find it necessary to put a sign saying "Emergency Exit" above a door?

'If there was a fire, I would see wall, gap, wall. I am Irish; I would aim for the gap.'

We had some interesting moments as well. In Brighton the arrival of a parcel of new shirts from his tailor which was addressed to him, care of me, caused a security incident at my hotel.

We were playing the Dome Theatre, which is a beautiful building that originally was the stables for the Brighton Pavilion. Brighton was on high alert as the Conservative Party Conference was being held at the same time as our visit and the party's hotel, the Grand, had been bombed by the Provisional IRA four years previously on 12 October 1984.

All hotels at the time had a policeman 'in residence' in reception and of course this parcel with Dave's name on it caused consternation and a lot of questions. I arrived just in time to stop the hotel being evacuated and probably the destruction of the parcel and all because of Dave's shirts.

There were some 'odd' times as well. Dave was playing

the Theatre Royal in Glasgow. It is a very beautiful theatre, but somehow at the time we all felt we didn't fit in. The noise boys were the first to spot it, then Dave and I as Dave was offered a tiny, chocolate-coloured, dark dressing room, which seemed to be round the corner, down the stairs and miles away.

During the day there were performances of *Postman Pat* for children, and even Dave picked up that, although everyone was nice to us, there was a tangible gap. It didn't help that our hotel was a little strange as well and very much a second choice for Dave. We had been pipped to the post at the hotel he had hoped to stay at by an international golf tournament. We were in what would now be called a 'boutique hotel', except that Dave had been put in a converted mews house that was stuck in the sixties, complete with lemon bathroom, wrought-iron railings, on a duplex-type level and black and white tiles. I was hiding in my room that had a tartan carpet and tartan wallpaper when there was a knock on my door. It was Dave coming to see if I thought we should change hotels; he took one look at my room, roared with laughter and beat a hasty retreat to his retro-sixties chic mews cottage.

Whenever things weren't going as smoothly as we wanted I found that my dry-cleaning challenge became a lot more stressful. Dave was very particular about the finish of his suits, and with local places all around the UK at the time, it was very hit and miss. There wasn't only the problem of remembering to pick them up, especially if we were moving on, but there was also the stress of waiting for Dave's critical assessment of whether they had 'totally buggered up the lapels' or left a high shine on everything. It is interesting how things can suddenly become of huge importance when you are away from home for long periods. With Dave, it was his suits and hotel rooms.

The week in Glasgow was of course a sell-out, and the audience as usual enjoyed themselves, but I found myself doing the load-out at the end of the week by myself, lugging carpet, chair, etc. down flights of stairs, and our sound boys were left to their own devices as well. It was unusual and probably completely unintentional, but Dave remarked that he felt 'second class' at the theatre, even to *Postman Pat.*

Ian, our sound operator, had as dry a sense of humour as Dave, and when Dave asked him on the last day what he thought the problem was at the theatre, he just tapped his nose and said enigmatically, 'Masons,' to which Dave replied, 'Of course.' It sounded like a good reason at the time, although it was a joke and none of us knew what had actually gone on. We were really quite pleased to move on.

Dave had really been looking forward to the week in Aberdeen. I had never visited the 'Granite City' before, and we arrived just after the Piper Alpha disaster, which had caused the death of 167 men in July. The news was still full of it, and a lot of the people we met during our stay had personally been touched by the disaster. So many of the men who had died were from Aberdeen.

His Majesty's Theatre is very beautiful and welcoming, and our season went well, although Dave couldn't believe that the manager of the hotel, whom he was so looking forward to seeing again, was long gone and the hotel was a pale shadow of the place that he remembered.

There was a party for Dave arranged by the 'friends of the theatre' after the show one night. It was good fun. We were then left on our own to go back to the dressing rooms and find our way out of this silent, dark theatre.

As we were going from the bar in the front of house, an elderly man came to our rescue and took us along an underground passage to the way out. It was a long walk and rather spooky. Dave and I kept looking at each other as we had no idea where we were. As we approached the stairs and the exit door, we turned to say goodnight to our guide, but he had vanished. There was no other exit, and Dave shrugged and said, 'That must have been the theatre ghost.' It was funny but really baffling and quite frightening. We fast-walked up the hill and back to our hotel. Our ghost story stayed with us for the rest of the tour.

Our last night was in Sheffield at City Hall. Dr Oliver Double remembers seeing the show that night, 'I was watching from high up so I got this amazing view of a grey mass of hair nodding and bobbing around.

'There was a woman sitting next to me; she was with her husband. The first time that Dave swore, said "fuck", she was actually shocked. Then the next time he said it there was a frisson. Then finally she started to giggle but looked as if she really shouldn't be. It was fascinating to watch.'

Karin Stark came up on the last night to see Dave in Sheffield and wanted to surprise him. With a lot of awful ham acting on my part, I pretended that she was our stalker trying to get in to see Dave. He looked horrified as he saw me pretending to push someone away just outside his dressing-room door and was prepared to leap into action, but was then thrilled to see that it was in fact Karin.

Back home in London Dave hosted and cooked an end-of-tour meal for the promoters and me. This in itself was unusual and was really a wonderful gesture and a great meal. I hadn't expected anything like that and certainly did not expect a present of a beautiful pair of earrings from Dave. Luckily, I had thought of something for him. When we had been in Belfast, we had visited a children's charity. It was a promotional event for the charity, but we were shown some amazing photos that had been taken of the children and the charity's work and I asked them for one of the photos of a mother kissing a laughing baby for Dave. He hadn't remembered seeing it and was pleased. I told him that it had reminded me of one of his paintings. It seemed a paltry 'thank you' in return for all those meals, but he did seem pleased. The tour really had been an amazing experience. I was now heading back to the land of unemployment, acutely aware that I would probably never have the pleasure of working with someone as intelligent, astute, friendly and such great fun as Dave. We did meet again later of course; Dave and Karin came to see *Carmen*, which I was working on at Earls Court – although with typical candour Dave proclaimed it to be 'appalling' – then a few years later, at a José Carreras concert. Dave paid me a huge compliment by asking me to meet up with Jane, his daughter, and talk to her about stage management. She was at Mountview Theatre

School at the time, and having met her, I didn't think she needed any help or guidance from me as she was obviously going to be good at it.

After the UK tour Dave returned to Australia. The tour manager for this tour was Michael Condon, son of Patrick Condon, Dave's life-long friend. Michael Condon recalls, 'My "love affair" started with Dave when I was just four; you remember that he used to sit and tell us ghost stories and do the most incredible magic tricks imaginable. I still try to pull the burnt match head with the "magic" invisible string and still can't do it.

'Our families had been joined together since my dad met him in 1963. Edward and I are the same age, and whenever Jane or Edward came to Australia, they would stay with us, and we would do the same when we went to England. Dad and Dave used to call it "pay-back time". All the stories about Ed's sunburn that he got on the first day out in Australia once, the barbecues and stories of bacon and eggs would find their way into Dave's shows. And then later Karin would willingly put up with this extended family of Dave's. We have had some great times.

'I was Dave's tour manager in 1989, and we started in Perth. We had flown from Sydney with one of the production team, John Winchcomb. John is a bearded burly-looking character who could consume large quantities of liquor. As I was an up-and-coming member of the team, I thought that it was essential that I match him drink for drink and of course this was Jack Daniels. Well, you know what they say about drinking and flying – that one in the air is worth two on the ground – and by the time we landed in Perth I was completely smashed.

'When we landed, in my emboldened state, I assumed the role of Dave's personal bodyguard and was clearing a path for Dave through the terminal buildings like he was a rock star. Dave Allen just told everyone that we passed that I was a "perverted faggot". You can imagine how much he was enjoying all this.

'John Thornton was our local agent and he had met us at the airport with two cars, except I didn't realise that he actually worked for us. I just assumed that we were going to be ripped off by a local taxi driver. I went on and on at him in the cab, drunk still of course, and completely ignored Dave telling me that he worked for us. I was apparently using every obscenity under the sun and even threatened him with his life if he didn't take us on the most direct route. I then jumped over the seat at one point and tried to put him in a headlock. I am not proud of this story, but you can imagine how Dave built this up each time he told it. It was hysterical and it is the story that I wanted Dave to tell at my eventual wedding.

'Dave had some good touring companions at this time. We were following Chris de Burgh everywhere, and the two of them, being both Irish of course, met up by the hotel pools in all the cities we went to. They had long hours together.

'We went on to Adelaide next, and apart from Dave being a great success there as usual, the tour was sponsored by

Andrew Garrett with his wines, so this stay was memorable for the lunches at his winery.

'It sounds like nothing but great meals, good company and drinking, but there were the shows to do and nothing was ever straightforward. During the tour through Northern Queensland there were floods all over the state. John Winchcomb and I would drive between cities as we were doing one-night stands at the time, so we drove through the night after the show and Dave flew.

'Between Gladstone and Gympie the highway was closed. This meant we had some serious off-roading to do in the middle of the night. It was one of those journeys that you never forget, with us having to stop every couple of miles to use winches and pulleys to get us out of mud holes. There was a moment when we thought we weren't going to make it to Gympie for the show.

'By the time we got there we were exhausted, covered in mud and very late. John and I were flying round the theatre, doing the lighting, sound checks and making sure everything was ready for Dave.

'We collected Dave from his hotel and John took him to the theatre. I was out in the town trying to find Moët & Chandon and J&B in a small Ozzie country town, which was not easy. Then it hit me that I hadn't got his suits dry-cleaned.

'I got to the theatre, and he looked at me and he just lost it, saying that I was a "fucking idiot" and that I only "had one thing to do" and that was to get his suits cleaned. By the time I had explained that John and I were lucky to get there, but that I was sorry about his suits, he just stood there, in his underwear, calling me a stupid dickhead with that famous half finger sticking in the air! I took a photo of him leaning against a breeze-block wall in his underpants with that finger up at me. He always wondered why I had taken that photo, but it is a good memory.

'I think he set all of us up to fail with the dry-cleaning business. You could never get it right, or rather the dry-cleaners could never get it right.'

The 'Tarzan' of old came to Michael's rescue on one of their 'scenic route' journeys when they weren't on a deadline: 'Dave saved my life in Darwin. We were visiting a crocodile park and we stopped by what looked like a peaceful billabong with a fence round it. I took a photo of it and dropped my lens cap through the fencing.

'I climbed over the fence to get the lens cap back, and Dave suddenly saw this bubbling and boiling in the water and realised that it was a croc coming to get me. Dave was screaming and abusing me; I hadn't seen the croc, and he was telling me to get out of there. I just made it as an attendant threw the croc a lump of chicken. If Dave hadn't had such quick reactions and started shouting, I wouldn't have made it.

'We met so many people on this tour. In Brisbane Sir Peter Ustinov was playing at the Queensland Performing Arts Centre, and it was a very special moment with both of these people playing in the same venue. I spent the evening as the drinks waiter, hopping between the two dressing rooms, listening to the banter and the stories.

'In Melbourne we stayed at the Hilton on the Park, with frequent visits to the Shark Fin restaurant on Little Collins

Street up the road. Dave was playing His Majesty's Theatre to sell-out crowds as usual.

'During one of my many flights on that tour I had befriended a group of Ansett airhostesses, and Dave made me look so good in front of them. Whenever we met up, I would invite them to dinner, and Dave would mutter and mumble, begrudgingly hating the fact that he would always have to pay for them all, but you knew he loved it. He enjoyed the company of different people so much.

'Our tour continued, and in Sydney he played the Seymour Centre, and the stay was highlighted by an eventful evening in a Chinese restaurant called the Golden Century. The guests included Lady Susan Renouf, Patrick Hockey, the artist who sadly died in 1992, and the Australian movie star Jack Thompson [who played Cliegg Lars in *Star Wars* among many other roles], and my dad, Pat, was there of course as well.

'The Golden Century was at that time a hole-in-the-wall type of place, where if you didn't speak Chinese, it was difficult to get served. This was a great challenge for Dave and he loved it. By the end of the meal he had all the staff eating out of the palm of his hand.

'It was an incredible meal which ended up with Patrick Hockey and Dave taking all the clutter off the table and turning the tablecloth into this huge piece of art. Everyone piled in and drew on it as well. Between the soy-sauce stains and the wonderful artwork by Patrick and Dave it was really stunning.

'Dave finished the evening by walking out of the restaurant wrapped in this tablecloth, wearing it like a toga. We were all saying our goodbyes in the restaurant when we caught a glimpse of Dave out on the pavement. He looked like the second coming, with his long, grey-white hair and that toga.

'As we went out to join him, the gradient of the road proved too much for Dave and over he went. We all got to him in time to see him lying there like a large white slug. His arms were trapped inside the cloth, and he was shouting at us that we were all … well, you can imagine!

'My dad still has that tablecloth as a work of art!

'Sadly the last part of the tour came round all too quickly for me. We were in Darwin, and on our last night we were invited to the Paspaleys' [famous for their pearls] residence for a great cocktail party then returned to our hotel for a late-night sauna session. Most hotels shut their saunas at 10 p.m. so this was always a challenge for me and the hotel management to keep them open for Dave Allen.

'That night, as a celebration for the last night of a very successful tour, we ordered in a couple of bottles of Moët & Chandon and sat drinking stark naked in the spa. Looking back, this was a very special moment.

'Dave started to get an Aboriginal chant going. John Winchcomb and I joined in, adding our own clapping and vocal arrangements to it. It lasted for about thirty minutes. It was really a very spiritual moment. Dave cared a lot about the Aborigines in Australia. He loved their painting as well and knew a couple of the more famous Aboriginal artists. Dave and I had spent many hours arguing and discussing the Aborigines' situation in Australia. It was really a fitting end to the tour and for our last drink together.

Dave Allen left a successful tour for home. With good reviews from Australia and New Zealand and the earlier rough ones from the UK, he had a lot to think about. His style of humour was still successful, and live audiences still craved it, even though the critics now considered him to be 'old hat' compared to the 'new' alternative comics. But he had worked out what he thought was necessary to put him back in the forefront of people's minds, and presumably, he hoped his next move would act as a wake-up call to the supposed competition and any doubters about his ability.

CHAPTER SEVEN

A VERY IRISH RETIREMENT

In 1990, in another change of style and direction but possibly the one which would have the most impact, Dave Allen brought his stage show to our television screens.

The sketches were never part of his stage show, but the stories were, and now, never afraid to take risks, he was going to bring the show that had entertained thousands of people around the world for years into millions of homes, complete with the 'rage', the humour and the language. After four years away from the UK's television screens Dave Allen was about to return to the BBC with a vengeance.

The first episode of *Dave Allen* was broadcast on BBC1 on Saturday 6 January at 10 p.m. He started with a description of his life to date. He said that he was retired, but in order to keep himself in the manner to which he had become accustomed, he had to work. He called it an Irish sort of retirement.

The show was of course very funny and took everyone through the process of ageing, what happens to your skin and memory and on through tales of anger and frustration. This was an older and apparently angrier Dave Allen. He seemed to spend more time searching for the 'cue' word. There was a lot of repetition at the start of the main gags that led into the stories. I wondered if he had abandoned the idiot cards as he hadn't used them on stage in a theatre. It was not as tight a show as it used to be, but it was extremely funny.

Twenty-eight minutes into the show the switchboard of the BBC was jammed with complaints. Dave Allen had told a story. It was merely an observation about an everyday object told with Dave Allen style, but it caused an enormous furore.

'We live our lives by the clock. We are taught to revere and respect the clock, or time. You wake to the clock; you go to work to the clock. You clock-in to the clock. You clock-out by the clock. You come home to the clock. You eat to the clock. You drink to the clock. You go to bed to the clock. You go back to work to the clock.

'You do that for forty years of your life. You retire and what do they fucking give you? – a clock.'

While the studio audience was in hysterics, the switchboard at the BBC was reportedly inundated with calls about the use of that one word, 'fucking'.

Three days later, on 9 January, the BBC issued an apology. The Corporation said that a warning should have been issued. Mr Robert Haywood, the then Conservative MP for Kingswood in Bristol tabled a Commons question to the

Home Secretary of the time, David Waddington, asking him to discuss the issue with the BBC.

After a twenty-eight-minute programme full of the usual stage-show verbal arsenal of 'arseholes', 'shit', 'dickheads' and 'crap', it was interesting that one word could cause so much offence. As Dave told everyone, they should know what to expect with him.

In an interview with Valerie Grove of the *Sunday Times*, Dave said, 'I have been performing on television for twenty-five years. People know what I am about. They know what I am and what I do. If people are going to be startled by me then they don't watch.' Grove reports that he was 'surprised but not contrite. He [Dave] had recorded an hour which had been edited down to thirty minutes. They didn't even discuss the offending word on a show going out at the post-curfew hour of 10 p.m.'

James Moir was head of light entertainment at the time. 'You have to take yourself back to 1990. Although it wasn't the first time the word had been broadcast, with hindsight I probably should have put out a warning before the show was aired. As a public broadcasting service we had a duty to watch out for anything like that.

'In the edit suite we had cut quite a few "fucks" and "fuckings", and this was the one that stayed. It was plea-bargaining with Dave, if you like: "If we drop four, you can keep one." And that was the one that survived.

'Dave had made a decision that this was the way he wanted his shows to go. He wanted to cross boundaries or frontiers. I informed the controller and that was it.

'Of course the press had a field day with it all,' which was what Dave Allen had hoped for to get rid of the 'old-fashioned, Val Doonican' Dave Allen and update himself in the only way he knew how.

Barry Cryer said, 'Dave was very adamant about keeping the words in. He could dig in his heels when he wanted to, and as I said, it was all performer driven. The plea-bargaining was just like the stories that Frank Muir used to tell about working on shows like *Till Death Us Do Part* where you could have two "bloodys" but you had to get rid of the "other" bit.'

Dave Allen had attempted to beat his perceived competition at their own game to update his show and his image. Dave spent the rest of the year working and planning for a tour to New Zealand with shows that would contain the same language that he had used on his BBC series. He returned to New Zealand in November 1990, but this time, on his last visit, only played five venues: Christchurch, Wellington, Auckland, Hamilton and Palmerston. It would be his last visit there and was highly successful.

He returned to England to commence a season at the Strand Theatre. He opened on 14 February. As usual the whole season was a sell-out before the show even opened. Obviously the viewers who had complained to the BBC were not going to venture to the show, but the publicity generated in the months before would certainly have boosted any sales, had that been necessary.

André Ptaszynski, then of Pola Jones the promoters, remembers, 'Dave was sold out at the Strand weeks before it opened so he decided that there was no reason to keep any tickets back for the critics. This was unheard of in the West

End. All the critics would expect complimentary tickets for the show. There is a whole routine of them having their favourite drinks, favourite seats, etc. But Dave decided that they weren't invited and if they wanted to come and cover the show, then they had to buy their tickets, like everyone else. It caused a great hullabaloo.

'But by this stage, you know, he really didn't care. He was what I call "harvesting" – buying property and setting himself up for retirement. But he could have easily gone on for another ten years.'

Writer and comic Barry Cryer remembered, 'My wife and I went out for a meal with Dave after the show at the Strand, and at the time I hadn't done any one-man shows. I was stunned at how he could be on stage for over two hours. I was also surprised at the language. But he was way ahead of people like Billy Connolly with his "rage" and "anger" about subjects. He never wanted to be the same as everyone else and it worked.'

The rage and anger that was portrayed on stage was rarely seen in the private Dave Allen. His storytelling had completely evolved from the comedian telling amusing stories to become a true actor's performance. While he could have as little patience or as much indignation as anyone, when faced with something or someone ludicrous, he was quiet, observant and non-committal until pushed.

Barry Cryer continued, 'During the meal I asked him how he managed to sustain the show night after night as it must have been exhausting. He said that it was just "four bits". I laughed at him at this description of "four bits". But after analysing the show, he was right. Even if the "four bits" are never the same twice, it worked. He always knew where he was in the "bit", and although there were other bits and pieces, he was right.

'I now go on the road with my own show and always think of Dave as I do my "four bits", and it isn't exhausting. Sure, it's not easy, but he put it all into perspective for me.'

Dave had always wanted to make another documentary. Over the years there had been ideas for programmes about second-generation blacks in England; then he wanted to return to Ireland to make a film about the River Boyne, near his home in Firhouse.

When he went to present the idea for a documentary on the down-and-outs on the River Boyne, the BBC didn't know exactly what to do with him or his idea. Maybe it was too soon after the clock incident, or maybe the people there also believed that he was old-fashioned. There was also the possibility that they had no idea that he had ever done anything other than the type of show they had seen in 1990. André Ptaszynski said, 'Like a lot of people, Dave fell out of favour with the BBC at that time. There had been a lot of changes in the staff and leadership.'

It must have been a blow to the man who for decades could walk into any television station and propose a show, or who could pick which channel to go to next when something had not gone as smoothly as he wanted.

Valerie Wilson, a PA on his shows, commented, 'It's so very sad that, like so many talented artists, he seemed to become increasingly bitter towards the end of his time at the BBC.'

Dave settled down to a routine at home, doing the

gardening, looking at scripts and proposals, thinking about work and screaming at the local kids to stop them playing football outside his house. He described himself to journalists as becoming the archetypal grumpy old man.

In 1992 the entertainer Roy Castle died of lung cancer. He had campaigned for cancer charities for weeks when he was very ill. The cause of his cancer, he believed, was due to passive smoking. As he had never smoked, he believed it was due to the smoke that he had inhaled during the years when he toured the club circuit with his act.

André Ptaszynski remembered, 'We were at a dinner party that Dave was giving at his house. It was just after Roy Castle had died. Dave was a superb cook and always produced a fabulous curry. We had all been drinking well. It was as usual a great evening with Dave.

'The subject went round to Roy Castle, and out of the blue Dave suddenly announced that passive smoking was why he had emphysema – from inhaling passively all the smoke when he was on the club circuit, just like Roy Castle.

'We were all dumbstruck at first, then I think it was my wife, Judith, who said, "So all those cigarettes for all those years don't count then, Dave?" She was half-joking, of course, but it was what we were all thinking.

'He ignored her totally. I am certain that if you had shown him one of the early videos of him smoking through his act, he would not have seen the cigarette. None of us knew that Dave had this as well or how long he had been suffering from it.'

Michael Sharvell-Martin could not remember a moment

in the beginning 'where Dave didn't have a cigarette; even when he was eating he always had one clamped between his fingers near his knife'.

André Ptaszynski continued, 'He compartmentalised everything, and I am certain he did that with the smoking. My children went to the Dragon School, near Oxford, same as his son, Edward. We were talking one day at the school, and he started to talk about Judith, his ex-wife. He stopped dead and you could see him shut it away. He did that with a lot of things.'

When he had 'just stopped' smoking, friends thought at the time that he may have had hypnotherapy because they could not otherwise understand how he had broken such a serious habit of a rumoured eighty-Gauloises a day for at least twenty years. Hypnotherapy could also explain how he could just ignore cigarettes, perhaps even that he had been convinced during his therapy, and as part of the cure, that he had never smoked. However, it was emphysema that would eventually claim the life of Dave Allen.

Given Dave's apparent ill health, nobody was surprised when Dave appeared on television again with almost the same show. In 1993 he was with Carlton Television on ITV and was promoted as 'uncensored'. Fired up by the hype that preceded the series and heavy expectation that he would really be pushing the limits, the critics were quick to point out that he hadn't put in any new material and, although 'uncensored', the word 'fucking' did not appear in this series. Whatever the critics thought, however, the series won him the 'Best Comedy Performer' at the British Comedy Awards.

During 1994, the *Sydney Morning Herald* reported on another Allen on their shores. There was quite a hint of her father, Dave Allen, in the paper's short gossip piece about Jane. On 5 October 'Jane, daughter of the Irish comedian Dave Allen, arrived here last week as stage manager of the production of *Turandot* in the football stadium. To help her recover from the flight, she was whisked up to bone-dry Gumin Gumin station, on the fringe of the Warrumbungles. From there on Friday night, she reported by phone to her father in London on the state of our drought.

'Meg Mather-Brown, of Gumin Gumin, tells us that Mr Allen helpfully did a rain dance at the other end of the phone. Result: Gumin Gumin 2 mm, and in London a downpour.'

In 1994, on 26 December, Carlton broadcast a forty-five-minute special of *Dave Allen*, at 10.30 p.m. Once again the critics said that it held few surprises. People say that comedy had been fast-moving and evolving in style since the late eighties, and the critics perhaps appeared to think that Dave Allen had had his time. André Ptaszynski disagreed, 'We [Pola Jones] would have taken Dave Allen out on tour at any time and he would have sold out. His style of comedy just doesn't die. Even though he hadn't got any new material, I did speak to him about going out on tour again.

'I phoned him up and suggested that we meet, and instead of arranging to meet me in the office – this would have been around 1994 – Dave said that we should meet actually in the swimming pool of the Meridien Hotel in Piccadilly in London. With anyone else this would have been outrageous, but with Dave it was hilarious and just Dave being Dave.

Usually with these sorts of meetings, you meet at the office, you go through all the benefits to the artists about getting out in front of their fans, being accessible, keeping their name going and of course the money. Then you make suggestions for dates and venues, that sort of thing. It is a serious business meeting. But not with Dave.

'I met him in the pool, and we both bobbed up and down for a few lengths with me trying to ask him about his ideas for the tour and then just as I asked him a vital question about whether he would consider it or not, he would turn and off he went doing front crawl to the other end of the pool. It was very funny but a complete waste of time. He wasn't even remotely interested and never had been – he was just having fun with me.'

Although not working, Dave and Karin were seeing a lot of shows and watching the comics and the talent that were in England at the time.

André Ptaszynski remembers going up to the Edinburgh Festival with Dave in 1995 and a meeting with the then up-and-coming comic Alan Davies, 'Dave and I had gone up to Edinburgh to see who was performing that year. There is that great story about "handing over the sword", to someone who is coming along behind you that you think is worthy of it. Sir Laurence Olivier had been asked who he was going to hand the sword to, and he famously replied, "There isn't anyone."

'Dave and I sat at a table chatting with Alan Davies. Of course the first part of the conversation was dominated by Dave who kept on about how their names were the same but the other way round. He went on and on about

Dave Allen and Alan Davies, but then he started to talk to Alan about technique, timing, all sorts of things, and it reminded me of the "sword" story because it was as though Dave was handing all his knowledge and his place on the stage to Alan. Alan went on to develop the acting side of his career, though, but it was incredibly generous of Dave.'

In 1996, on 1 December at the London Television Centre, Dave Allen was awarded a 'Lifetime Achievement Award' at the British Comedy Awards.

Dave had worked a lot with charities over the years and in 1996 donated a picture for an auction, along with Sir Hugh Casson among others, to the Tricycle Theatre for Paint Box, an art project for children. He really had settled into his retirement and was not really looking for work but was happy to help wherever he could.

These true retirement years of Dave Allen had some high spots for his friends. Simone Condon remembers some great holidays with Dave and Karin during the 1990s: 'Dad and I joined Dave and Karin in the south of France in Lauris, in Provence. Dave was in charge of the red wine and the cooking. The most strenuous thing any of us did was going into town to do the shopping.

'Neither Dad nor Dave spoke French. They spent their time going round making up their own language, of course in hysterics at their own jokes and confusing the locals and Karin and me. They were very funny to watch, like kid brothers misbehaving.

'We went on to Portugal as well near Albufeira. We had loads of sun, reading, eating and drinking; it was sangria this time. We never did anything strenuous. Dave loved to cook for all of us so that was a big part of the day.

'He was so generous with his time and his care for all of us. Dave was terrible first thing in the morning; he used to get up very late, and we would creep around trying not to disturb him.

'But the day I flew in from Australia to Heathrow with my boyfriend, he was there at Heathrow at 6 a.m. That was unbelievable for him. He and Karin even gave me a key to come and go as I pleased, and he insisted that my boyfriend came and stay as well.

'I learned very quickly that you couldn't come to the house without a bottle of J&B; it was a tradition. While I was staying with both of them, Dave put together a special for the BBC and had a DVD made of his favourite bits. It was wonderful to watch.'

In 1997 the show that Simone had watched Dave work on while she was in London was shown on BBC1 in six parts, introduced by Dave and called *The Unique Dave Allen*. It would be the last time that we would see any version of the Dave Allen shows but wasn't his last television appearance.

While there weren't any new shows from Dave, it was surprising that new specials hadn't been compiled and shown on either channel. But everyone who worked with Dave knew about his tight editorial control of his shows. Michael Sharvell-Martin had seen how Dave reacted to the editing of the US versions of his show: 'It took years to persuade Dave to release the videos of the shows. He was really against it as he was angry at the way the shows had been edited for the US market. Minutes had been lopped off certain pieces and sketches, and the timing gone from lots of sections to allow for the commercial breaks in the US.

'When the first video was finally released, it was an incredible success. We all were getting something like eleven pence a video, so I was astonished to receive a royalty cheque for £10,000. That is a lot of video sales. The second one was sold on by the BBC to another company, and even though it outsold the first video, somehow instead of receiving £15,000 we all got £300. That's life, I suppose, but it shows the market for Dave, which I believe still exists.

'Everyone wanted to see Dave Allen then and would love to see him now, but Dave retained the editorial control of all the programmes, and I am certain that now he is dead, they will not be shown. It is a great shame and all apparently because of the American editing.'

Dave Allen hadn't yet disappeared from our British television screens completely however, and he appeared as himself as a commentator or a guest on various programmes, including in 1998 *Bring Me Sunshine: The Heart and Soul of Eric Morecambe* on BBC1, on *Clive Anderson All Talk*, also shown on BBC1, and in 1999 in *Tobacco Wars*, a BBC TV documentary (three episodes). The latter was a programme with the television journalist Michael Buerk among others. His last radio interview, on BBC Radio 4, was in 1999.

In 2000 he appeared on *Stand Up with Alan Davies* on the BBC. At the end of the year Dave would find that he was the sole surviving brother of the three boys who got into so much mischief in Firhouse. On 6 December his brother

Peter died, away from the limelight. He had retired, having worked his way up the career ladder in journalism to become the editor of the *Irish Times*. Peter's widow survives him. By this time Dave's mother had also died, but the date of her death is unclear.

Dave's love of painting and helping charities persisted, and in 2001 he supported Marie Curie Cancer Care with an exhibition of his paintings. Otherwise, Dave's retirement continued, and while Karin was working as a theatre producer herself, Dave was content to stay at home.

In 2004 Dave Allen married Karin Stark, his girlfriend of some seventeen years. Independent, with a career of her own as a theatre producer she had always been there for Dave. Friends in Australia were thrilled when Karin became pregnant as they had been 'trying for years'. People were concerned though when phone calls and messages began to be ignored and arrangements for meals were not followed through. The highly social Dave Allen was not seen around as often as he had been, and twelve years after announcing at a dinner party about his illness, in December 2004 he was reported to be 'quite ill' from his emphysema.

CODA

'MAY YOUR GOD...'

Kensington High Street in West London is always busy. Set just beside Knightsbridge, it is a smart part of London with large department stores, and in the past it was the land of Biba and smart and extremely trendy boutiques.

In one part of the area are hugely expensive pillared houses set discreetly back in tree-lined avenues. It is the land of embassies. There is the odd royal palace as well, two beautiful parks and some very expensive hotels.

Regular drivers and locals know the back doubles, the 'rat-runs' to avoid the lights and the congestion. They are trying to escape Notting Hill Gate at one end and then the junction at the end of Kensington Church Street, where it meets Kensington High Street.

One Thursday night, 10 March 2005, they found one of their escape routes completely blocked and they were going nowhere. The narrow road with cars parked on both sides was barricaded that night with ambulances. They couldn't get past. The cars sat patiently and the queue got longer.

Neil Michael reported for *Ireland on Sunday*, 'Face framed by a shock of grey hair, the old man would launch angry rants at the children playing outside the window of his book-lined front room. The only clue to his identity was the finger that he wagged at the tearaways, as the bottom two joints were missing. For the epitome of the grumpy old man was Dave Allen.

'Allen ventured out from his house ever more rarely. His final night out came when he dined out at The Terrace restaurant close to his home.

'On Thursday night the ambulance was called by anxious relatives who had been unable to raise Allen on the telephone. The crew found the sixty-eight-year-old slumped in a seat.

'Everyone in the street knew who lived there. His neighbours described him as the original "grumpy old man". They called him a recluse who never left the house. A "grumpy old fart" said one of the boys who lived next door, who Dave used to scream at for playing football outside his house, a man who gazed out of the window of his house, just looking.

On Thursday 10 March Dave Allen, the father of stand-up comedy, died, slumped in his chair. It didn't seem right that he hadn't died ranting on stage, making the audience howl with laughter. Instead he did it 'backstage', without an audience. With only a tiny percentage of his lung capacity left, the emphysema had apparently caused heart failure.

When the news broke the next morning that this much-loved comedian had died, the messages flooded in to the television stations and newspapers. The story was unusually headlined all day, not just at lunchtime.

As Henry Kelly wrote in *Ireland on Sunday*, 'He would have liked the irony of his death being announced on Red Nose Day.' [A biennial day-long event for the charity Comic Relief.]

His death caught everyone by surprise and people were left with a feeling of unfinished business and that Dave Allen had so much more to give us. Everybody felt that he was 'no age' to die.

Patrick Condon remembered the exact moment that he heard about Dave's death, 'Ed [Dave's son] phoned me to tell me the dreadful news. I was in China and just putting my key-card in the door of my hotel room. When he finished telling me, I just collapsed on the end of the bed and wept.

'I had lost my best friend, my adviser and personal entertainer who had been part of my life since 1963. I flew straight back but then found that the funeral had been changed and I would miss it. I have never really got over the fact that I couldn't say goodbye to him. I sat talking to Karin and helping her; it was all I could do and the least I could do for my friend, but I really miss him; he will always be with me.'

Michael Condon remembered, 'I have a lot to thank Dave Allen for. I have to thank Dave for teaching me how to open a bottle of champagne correctly and for letting me gain fourteen pounds in three months while we were out on the road.

'He taught me how to eat well and, of course, drink well. He never let me pay for anything while working for him, just as he did with you and everyone who was in his company. He taught me how to find a good dry-cleaner, although I don't think he was ever happy with any of them. He taught me how to tell a good story, so I learned from the master, Dave Allen. You cannot get better than that. He taught me how to deal with a whisky-induced hangover.

'He taught me how to appreciate weeds in the garden that he would never cut or mow. His garden in Kensington was like a jungle. He taught me how to have a good laugh. I have to thank him for the memories of discussions or arguments that you could never win, even if you were right. I have to thank him for introducing me to some fascinating people.

'I have to thank him for making me and millions of people laugh and look at language and the world in a completely different way. I have to thank him for being a good friend to me, my dad, Simone my sister and for looking after all of the family.'

Simone, Michael's sister, said, 'I was in Brisbane in March when he died. As you know, I called him my surrogate dad. He always helped me with problems, career advice or would just be there to have a yarn to. Everyone in my family will miss him hugely.'

Barry Cryer said, 'I heard about his death with the phone call that everyone dreads. I had just finished a show in Nottingham and took a call from BBC news. It was those dreadful words that go, "Don't know if you've heard but..."

Of course, like everyone, after the shock and the sorrow the guilt kicks in. Peter Vincent and I had said only a couple of weeks earlier, "Must go and have lunch with Dave." Peter had phoned him, and Dave had said, "Sure, plenty of food in the house." But we didn't.'

'I happened to hear a programme on BBC Radio Four at the end of February where everyone was eulogising about Dave. I was so very pleased for him and remember thinking, "About time,"' said Michael Sharvell-Martin. He continued, 'But it sounded like an obituary the way everyone was going on. I phoned him up and left a message on his machine saying, "What's happened? Have you died or something?! Just heard this programme on the radio and is there anything you want to tell us?" He didn't call me back, and the next thing is of course that he died just a fortnight later.

'I bet he is up there on his cloud, J&B in hand, having a great laugh at that, muttering, "Timing, Michael, timing."'

For over thirty years Dave Allen had been an institution on British, New Zealand and Australian television, in fact anywhere around the world where they showed his programmes. His shows became programmes 'not to be missed' and were talked about for days afterwards. Dave Allen had always dared to do something different, to challenge boundaries, and apart from in his own words, 'never wanting to hurt anyone', he really didn't care what people thought.

From the moment he sat on a stool, with his glass of J&B and a Gauloise cigarette, he was creating a new genre of comic, an observer who drew on his father's storytelling to spin yarns and go on to create hysterical, sometimes incredibly subtle sketches. Even though he had inherited most of his father's skills, he managed to avoid the apparently irresistible lure of alcohol and gambling that had dogged his father and his brother, Johnny, but still enjoyed all of it.

Dave Allen drew on his experiences of watching people and on stories from his school friends about the Catholic Church, and he used his own imagination to create what that actually would be like. A subtle combination of extremely funny and dour, he didn't tolerate fools gladly. He was generous to a fault with friends and anyone working with him; he was, though, an astute businessman, extremely careful with money. He was very adept at working his celebrity status and the system, along with the television stations that were so hungry to have him on 'their' side, though he would have hated to admit that he used his fame at all.

A friend of mine, Jane Fletcher, told me this story about the impact Dave Allen had on her family: 'My dad used to call Dave Allen his mate. They had never met of course, but it was part of the family routine on a Saturday night in the seventies to have what we called a "fuddle", a treat – sweets, drinks, maybe something special for supper – and then we would settle down and watch Dave Allen.

'My dad used to toast his friend Dave with a glass of Scotch. I used to sit between my mum and dad not really understanding what they were laughing about. It brings back such warm memories of the time.

'We emigrated to Australia and try as he could, my dad just didn't fit in. He wore the shorts but with a shirt and tie.

He drove the mandatory Holden estate car, but we had full Sunday roasts in thirty degrees, instead of "barbies".

'One night in Australia we were watching Dave Allen on television. My dad took one look at Dave and decided, right then, that we were off home, back to England. Dave Allen had such a strong effect on him; he represented so much to him.'

His legacy to comedy is outstanding. Dr Oliver Double said, 'Dave Allen is so underrated in my opinion as a comedian. Look how Dave Allen changed his routine over the years. He started out on that stool, using quick gags, then he slowed down, he became more laidback. Look at how he used all his props. He was made for television and the close-up shot. He was meticulous with his timing, even brushing imaginary ash off his sleeve or trouser leg, or taking a drink. By the time I saw him in Sheffield in 1989 he never used that chair; it was just there to remind everyone.

'I show all my students tapes of Dave Allen. Some of them are too young to have seen him, but when they watch him they can see just how good he was.'

Michael Sharvell-Martin said, 'Dave loved children. He invited my wife and the kids to his house and out into the garden that he called the "jungle", and we had an amazing afternoon.

'My daughters were quite young then, five and nine, and Dave adored them. It was pure anarchy when it came to Dave and kids. He covered Kate and Ellen's arms in strawberry jam and cream, put pepper in their hair and then drew all the way up their arms in felt pen. They had never seen adults behave like this. Linda and I sat thinking, "All those years of conditioning down the drain." It was very funny.'

Linda Sharvell-Martin continued, 'We were living in Somerset at that time, so the girls sat in the back of the car proudly displaying their arms that Dave Allen had drawn on all the way home. They refused to wash it off for days.'

'They still talk about it to this day,' added Michael.

Dave Allen told Robert Gore-Langton in the *Sunday Times* in February 1991, 'My childhood is trapped. I'm trapped in my relationship with my father when he died. I still relate to him as a twelve-year-old boy.

'The world has put pressures and parental responsibilities on me. I'm now the father of myself in a sense. I relate to my own childhood through my children. I haven't really changed. My school mac has grown shorter.'

On 17 April, just three weeks after his death, Karin gave birth to Dave's son, Culm. Friends in London were thrilled as they had been so concerned for her and the baby after the shock of Dave's death.

'Don't mourn for me now, don't mourn for me never, I'm going to do nothing for ever and ever.'

(The verse Dave Allen told a reporter that he would like on his tombstone.)

DIGITALES

'When people say, "You must be the Irish comedian with the missing finger," I reply, "No, I am the Irish comedian with nine and a half fingers."' Dave Allen.

This section could be called 'He told me that ...' It is all to do with the myth that surrounds Dave's finger, or lack of part of it, on his left hand.

In the tradition of Irish storytelling, and to preserve some mystery, who knows which tale, if any, is true.

'I lost the tip of my finger because I used to pick up my drink with my left hand when I was on stage and the tip of the finger was always in the alcohol. Over the years the alcohol gradually dissolved it.' As told to André Ptaszynski, Michael Condon, James Moir, Peter Whitmore and Barry Cryer.

'He lost it when he was an apprentice in a machine shop.' Warren Seal.

'He lost it in a shooting accident in Ireland.' Michael Sharvell-Martin and John Ammands.

'My father chopped it off as a punishment for picking my nose.' Dave Allen during most interviews.

'I was so poor, so hungry, that when I wiped my arse one day, my bum ate my finger it was so hungry.' As told to Edward O'Mahony (Allen) in Plymouth 1988.

'But the day he lost his finger, oh ... He came in with the hand bandaged up and then took it off and he made a big thing of it. Everybody gathered around and had a look at this finger. Whereas other children might have been afraid of it, or might have hid it away, he took it off and showed it to us. It was a kind of celebration. He had placed his finger in the large wheel outside the old mill and one of the kids had turned the wheel and chopped his finger off. He was proud of it. It made him a kind of a celebrity because he came in and showed it to us and took the bandage off. It didn't seem to worry him anyway. It happened in the month of June.' Paddy Egan.

'I know the real story and I am not telling anyone.' Patrick Condon.

'He was scratching his bum when he sneezed and snapped his finger off.' Michael Condon.

DAVE ALLEN'S EULOGY FOR
JOHN COLLINS, PRODUCER FOR CHANNEL NINE

Warren Seal: 'Dave wrote this eulogy for John when he died a while back and Dave was devastated that he couldn't get over to Australia for the funeral so he wrote this wonderfully funny and typically Dave eulogy. I think that we would all want to say to Dave what he says to John at the end of this.'

Dave Allen: 'I first met John Collins in 1963. I was working for Jack Neary and NLT Productions doing a show for Channel Nine, *Tonight with Dave Allen*. John was brought in as an auxiliary producer. We were all babes in the television business learning as we went along – good, exciting times. Along with Ken Hall, Bruce Gyngell and Jack Neary, John was one of the founding members of the television boom that hit Australia in the early sixties.

My early memories of John: small, round, very self-assured, even cocky, and I say that with a smile. He was always very dapper; he was given to wearing sweaters in pastel shades; he had the best suits in Sydney, and whoever cleaned his shoes must have spent hours on them – but it certainly wasn't him. He was most ambitious, determined, even tenacious, but he never lost his humility. He was

221

overly kind, especially when he didn't think you would notice.

He tried to give the impression of being a rough, tough, cynical Aussie who didn't suffer fools gladly (or in any other way for that matter), but in reality he was a big softy.

Some of the things I remember about John: his hatred and loathing of traffic jams. There was nowhere worse in the world that he could spend time. He would literally drive miles out of his way, crossing and re-crossing, in order to keep moving. And while in the car never wasting a moment – either shaving while driving or talking on the first mobile telephone I had ever seen, an enormous black gadget which to him was even more frustrating than the traffic jam because with all the turning and twisting he kept losing the signal. Memories of his very large glass filled with Australian (what else?) red wine or his beloved Pernod. Not forgetting a cigarette down to the end. He would light one, take two or three drags then stub it out in the ashtray. And by the time he had stubbed out the first the second cigarette was already in his mouth being lit. Wonderful lunches that became tea, became supper, became dinner and occasionally became breakfast.

John had a house in Pymble, a wonderful old Victorian house, and he had converted what had been the billiard room into a bedroom, a room panelled from floor to ceiling with also a panelled door. That was my bedroom for the night.

I woke in the darkness needing to find a bathroom. In the gloom and with all the panelling I couldn't find a door so I circumnavigated the room about five or six times, getting more desperate as I went till I eventually found the handle of the door. The corridor was as black as night so I continued to feel my way till I eventually found what I was looking for.

I now had to find my bedroom, and try as I might, it had totally disappeared. So I found a door and went in and got into a bed and went off immediately into a deep sleep. Finally when I awoke, can you image my surprise to find lying beside me fast asleep John's mother.

After that I took to calling John my son.

Thank you, John, for all the good memories; thank you, John, for all the good advice, and thank you, John, for all the good laughs.

Safe journey.

Dave Allen

KEY DATES IN THE LIFE OF DAVE ALLEN

Significant career dates and stage and television appearances (not exhaustive).

1936
6 July, Gilbert David Tynan O'Mahony born in Dublin.

1948
19 April, (Father) Gerard John Cullen Tynan O'Mahony, 'Pussy', general manager of the *Irish Times*, dies.

(Brother) John joins Independent Newspapers, Dublin.

(Brother) Peter joins the *Drogheda Argus*.

1954
Dave Allen joins the *Drogheda Argus*.

1955
Joins his brother, John, at Butlins as a camp host at Filey.

1956
Moves to Butlins in Skegness, then Margate.

1958
Moves to Butlins in Brighton.

1959

Appears on the ATV talent show *New Faces*.

1960

Joins Hedley Claxton's company at the Hoe Theatre in Plymouth (aged twenty-three) as second comedian.
George Lacey, the famous pantomime dame, is also in the company.

1962

On tour with Helen Shapiro.

1963

Compère of tour with the Beatles in the UK.

Agent signs him for tour in Australia.

Appears at the Silver Spade and Chequers in Sydney.

GTV 9 – *In Melbourne Tonight* appearance (historically known as *IMT*).

Channel 9 – *Tonight with Dave Allen*. Eighty-four episodes are shown of this television programme in Australia during the 1960s.

October, Eartha Kitt appears on the show and rumours start about their affair. Kitt stays at the Chevron Hilton in Sydney, and Dave admits that they are 'going steady'.

Appears in England on *Sunday Night at the London Palladium*.

November, knocks himself unconscious live on television in Australia.

1964

January, meets Judith Stott.

9 March, marries Judith Stott in Sydney.

Wins Logies for 'Most Popular Male' and 'Most Popular Programme' for *Tonight with Dave Allen*.

December, leaves Australia where hundreds of fans turn up to see him off.

1965

7 October to 16 December, appears on *The Val Doonican Show* on BBC1 for eleven editions.

Appears at the Showboat Theatre in London.

Six-week season at the Talk of the Town.

1966

July, daughter, Jane, born.

Stands in for Tony Hancock in Blackpool as compère on *The Blackpool Show*.

22 October to 14 January 1967, *The Val Doonican Show*, occasional appearances.

1967

June season at Chequers in Sydney.

5 March, ABC (an ITV company) pilot of *Around with Allen* screened in Midlands and north of England but not London. (Recorded in September 1966.)

Five-week tour of nightclubs and television appearances.

Hosts *Sunday Night at the London Palladium.*

Awarded the Variety Club of Great Britain's 'ITV Personality of 1967'.

9 July to 1 October, ITV series one of *Tonight with Dave Allen* broadcast, usually on Sunday nights at 11.05 p.m.

23 December, forty-minute Christmas special on ITV.

ITV tries to switch Dave's show with *The David Frost Show.*

1968
April to July, hosts *The Big Show*, a variety show on ATV (ITV). Guests include Kathy Kirby, Frank Ifield, Dave Clark Five, etc.

May, son, Edward, born.

8 June, *The Dave Allen Show* broadcast on BBC2. Fifty-minute special in colour, shown on Sunday at 10.35 p.m.

23 June , *The Dave Allen Show* broadcast on BBC2. Sixty-minute special in colour, shown on Sunday at 8.15 p.m.

29 September, series two of *Tonight with Dave Allen* broadcast on Saturday nights at 11.20 p.m. on ITV.

1969
11 October to 1 November, *The Dave Allen Show* shown on the BBC on Saturdays at 7.30 p.m. Ernest Maxim directs.

December, *Dave Allen in the Melting Pot*, a special shot in New York which made television history as it featured the first interview with men who were openly gay. Shown on ITV.

1970

The Australian movie *Squeeze a Flower* released. Directed by Marc Daniels and Charles Isaacs and starring Walter Chiari, Rowena Wallace, Sue Lloyd, Dave Allen and others.

8 July, ITV/Thames broadcasts the sixty-minute colour programme *Inside the Mind of Dave Allen*. Starring Dave Allen and Bob Todd.

1971

21 January to 1 April, *Dave Allen at Large* (series one) broadcast. Six forty-five-minute programmes broadcast fortnightly on Thursdays on BBC2 at 9.20 p.m. Main Cast included: Dave Allen, Ronnie Brody, Michael Sharvell-Martin, Jacqueline Clarke, Ian Burford, Chris Serle, Peter Hawkins, Simon Barnes, Robert East, Doran Goodwin, Susie Baker, Paul McDowell, Ralph Watson. (N.B. not all the above appeared in all the episodes or specials.) Writers: Dave Allen, Peter Vincent, Austin Steele, Ian Davidson. Producer: Peter Whitmore.

April, appears at the Talk of the Town in London.

18 September, live ninety-minute special for Nine network in Australia. Interviews Peter Cook and Dudley Moore and causes controversy by telling the producer to 'go masturbate' when he tells Dave to stop for a commercial break.

1972

Appears in first straight theatre role as Dr Daly in *A Pagan Place* by Edna O'Brien at the Royal Court in London. Directed by Ronald Eyre.

27 January to 6 April, series two of *Dave Allen at Large* broadcast. Six twenty-five minute episodes shown on BBC2 fortnightly on Thursdays at 9.20 p.m. Achieves biggest audience ever for BBC2.

1973

ABC lifts two-year ban on Dave Allen's live television performances.

Appears as one of the international line-up of stars for the opening of the Sydney Opera House.

Two specials for Australian television.

Tours New Zealand, visiting Auckland, Hamilton, Wellington and Christchurch. However, a plane strike curtails this four-day tour of NZ.

15 January to 26 March, series three of *Dave Allen at Large* shown on BBC2. Six forty-five-minute episodes are shown on BBC2 fortnightly on Mondays at 9.25 p.m.

November, appears as Mr Darling and Captain Hook with Maggie Smith in the Robert Helpmann production of *Peter Pan* at the London Coliseum.

1974

A Little Night Reading, an anthology of horror stories compiled by Dave, is published.

24 January, *Dave Allen Once Again*, a forty-five-minute special, is shown on BBC2 on Thursday at 9 p.m. This is a retrospective collection.

ITV series *Dave Allen in Search of Great British Eccentrics*.

Voted 'Top Foreign Television Star' in Denmark.

Tours New Zealand, visiting Christchurch (x 3), Ashburton, Queenstown, Invercargill, Dunedin, Twizel, Timaru, Auckland, Nelson, Blenheim, Wellington, Masterton, Wanganui, New Plymouth, Palmerston North, Dannevirke, Napier, Hastings, Gisborne, Tauranga, Auckland, Hamilton, and Rotorua.

1975

The Dave Allen Show in Australia broadcast (1975 to 1979) on Nine Network. Cast included: Tina Bursell, Gordon Chater, Carla Hoogeven, Judy Morris, Eric Oldfield, Carol Passmore, Martin Phelna.

Four fifty-minute programmes for Seven Network.

'Stripping Pope' sketch causes complaints in UK.

ABC broadcasts *A Salute to Lew Grade*, filmed in New York, starring Dave Allen alongside Tom Jones, Julie Andrews, Peter Sellers and John Lennon.

Tour of Australia to all major cities.

Five-week season in Hong Kong.

1976

April, thirty-five-minute special, entered for Montreux Festival on BBC2.

Nominated for an Emmy for the same programme.

18 October to 20 December, series five of *Dave Allen at Large* broadcast fortnightly on BBC2, mostly on Mondays at 8.15 p.m.

Appears with The Shadows, Johnny Mathis, Buster Bates and Jack Jones in a sell-out concert at Coventry Theatre (the Hippodrome).

1977
RTE bans his shows in Ireland.

1978
Ten-week sold-out season at the Vaudeville Theatre, London.

An Evening with Dave Allen breaks all box-office records at the Theatre Royal in Norwich.

1979
Appears on ITV in Alan Bennett's *One Fine Day* in the role of George Phillips.

Six-week season in Australia.

Short tour of UK (autumn).

1 October, returns to Dublin for the first time with his show.

26 December, forty-five-minute special shown on BBC1 on Wednesday at 9.40 p.m.

1980
Five-week tour of Australia.

3 June, performances in Hong Kong at City Hall.

Tour of New Zealand.

Separates from Judith, his wife.

1981

An Evening with Dave Allen season at the Theatre Royal, Haymarket, London.

Stops smoking.

20 April, *Dave Allen*, a fifty-minute special, broadcast on BBC1 on Monday at 10 p.m. 29 May, BBC2 shows a fifty-five-minute special on Friday at 9.30 p.m. Series ran from 1981 to 1990. Main Cast for *Dave Allen:* Dave Allen, Jacqueline Clarke, Michael Sharvell-Martin, Paul McDowell, Susan Jameson. Writers: Dave Allen, Peter Vincent, Ian Davidson, Penny Hallowes, Dick Vosburgh, Andrew Marshall, David Renwick, Andy Hamilton, Dick Fiddy, Mark Wallington. Director: Bill Wilson. Producers: Bill Wilson, Peter Whitmore, James Moir.

USA, the Wilbur Theatre, Boston, *An Evening with Dave Allen*, moving to the Booth Theatre, New York, on 21 September.

1982

Three-week season at the Palace Theatre, Manchester.

One week at the Birmingham Hippodrome.

1983

Divorce at High Court in London on the grounds that they had lived apart for over the mandatory two years.

Tours New Zealand to over twenty venues: Auckland, Christchurch, Ashburton, Timaru, Dunedin, Invercargill, Greymouth, Westport, Neslon, Wellington, Palmerston North, Wanganui, Masterton, Napier, Hamilton, Rotorua, Tauranga, Gisborne, New Plymouth and Whangaerei.

1984

26 December, BBC1 shows a fifty-minute special on Wednesday at 9.55 p.m.

Mary Whitehouse, founder of the Clean Up Television campaign complains about Dave Allen, his attacks on the Church and use of bad language.

1985

Son, Edward, expelled from Radlett College for smoking cannabis.

8 April, fifty-minute special broadcast on BBC1 on Monday at 10 p.m.

1986

January, brother, John, dies in a fall from a window.

October, returns to Sydney with *An Evening with Dave Allen* and tours Australia.

31 December, BBC1 broadcasts a fifty-minute special on Wednesday at 9 p.m.

Season of *An Evening with Dave Allen* at the Albery Theatre in London.

Season of *Dave Allen Live* at the Arts Theatre, London.

1987

March, appears on *Saturday View* at the invitation of Bishop Empey.

Appears on *The Celts* on BBC1 as himself.

1988

An Evening with Dave Allen tour of UK stage.

Appears on *An Audience with Victoria Wood* as himself on LWT/ITV.

1989

Returns to tour Australia for the first time since 1985. Venues include the York Theatre and the Seymour Centre in Sydney.

Two nights of *An Evening with Dave Allen* in Los Angeles.

1990

6 January to 10 February, BBC1 broadcast six thirty-minute episodes of *Dave Allen* on Saturdays at 10 p.m. On 6 January BBC1 receives complaints about his language and questions are asked in Parliament.

9 January, BBC issues apology to public.

Tours New Zealand to Christchurch, Wellington, Auckland Aotea Centre, Hamilton, Palmerston and then Australia.

1991

14 February, opens at The Strand Theatre in London.

Exhibition of paintings for Marie Curie.

1993

7 January to 18 February, ITV (Noel Gay Television for Carlton) shows six thirty-minute episodes on Thursdays at 9.30 p.m.

Wins 'Best Comedy Performer' at British Comedy Awards.

1994

26 December, forty-five-minute special broadcast on Monday at 10.30 p.m. on ITV (Noel Gay Television for Carlton).

1996

1 December, Dave Allen is awarded a 'Lifetime Achievement Award' at the British Comedy Awards at the London Television Centre.

1997

The Unique Dave Allen shown on BBC1.

1998

Appears on *Bring Me Sunshine: The Heart and Soul of Eric Morecambe* as himself on BBC1.

Appears on *Clive Anderson All Talk*, shown on BBC1, as himself.

1999

Appears on *Tobacco Wars*, a three-episode BBC TV documentary. Michael Buerke and others also feature.

2000

Stars on *Stand Up with Alan Davies* as himself.

6 December, brother, Peter, former editor of the *Irish Times*, dies.

2004

Marries Karin Stark.

2005

10 March, Dave Allen dies at his home in Kensington, London.

15 April, his son, Culm O'Mahony (Allen), born.

POSTSCRIPT ON THE FAMILY HOME AT CHERRYFIELD

The last listing for Mrs Tynan O'Mahony at Cherryfield was in 1955. Some believe the house was then auctioned off and bought by the state. What is certain is that a state training and development agency (a back-to-work scheme) took over the house and began a number of enterprise projects to restore the house to its former glory, but the house was never properly secured, and at some stage in the late seventies/early eighties there was a break-in and the house was set alight. Although still in the possession of the same company, it was decided that it would be too costly to rebuild the shell and a decision was taken to demolish it because of safety concerns. The house was pulled down in 1986 and all that remains are ruins. However, the original lane leading up to the house still exists and forms part of a series of paths in what is now the Dodder Linear Park. The area is still known as Cherryfield.

SOURCES

Only main sources have been included.

BOOKS

Harvey Crane, *Playbill* (MacDonald & Evans, 1980).

Oliver Double, *Stand-up! On Being a Comedian* (Methuen, 1997).

Michael Freedland, *Sophie: The Sophie Tucker Story* (The Woburn Press, 1978).

Tony Goodliffe, *Stars in My Eyes* (HarperCollins).

Mark Lewsohn, *Radio Times Guide to TV Comedy* (BBC, 2003).

Raymond Mander and Joe Mitchenson, *The Theatres of London* (New English Library Times Mirror, 1975).

Michael J Newman, *The Golden Years: The Hippodrome Theatre, Coventry.* (Baron, 1995).

Philip Norman, *SHOUT! The True Story of the Beatles* (Sidgwick & Jackson, 2003).

Sue Read, *Hello Campers! Celebrating Fifty Years of Butlins* (Bantam Press, 1986).

Brian Rix, *Tour de Farce* (Hodder & Stoughton, 1992).

Gus Smith, *Dave Allen, God's Own Comedian* (Robert Hale, 1991).

INDEX

204; British Comedy Awards, 'Lifetime Achievement Award' 207; Emmy 144; Logie for 'Most Popular Male' 97; Silver Rose, Montreux 144; 'Top Foreign Television Star' in Denmark 135; Variety Club 'ITV Personality of the Year' 106; books: *A Little Night Reading* 134; children: Culm 218; Edward 25, 65, 107, 157, 164, 182, 190, 204, 219; Jane 25, 103, 157, 164, 189–90, 205; Jonathan Stott 96, 98, 100; drinking: alcoholics 111, 181; champagne 4, 7, 12–13, 16–17, 27, 98, 109, 117, 125, 129, 137, 159, 175, 181, 183, 213; 'a drinking man' 130, 132, 203, 216; Guinness 109; J&B 2, 4, 7, 27, 183, 192, 208, 215; sangria 207–8; family *see* Tynan O'Mahony; finger (missing) 2, 42, 54–5, 65, 182, 193, 220; generousity (financial

and professional) 63, 95, 136, 207, 208, 216; homes: Cherryfield 33–5, 43; Devon 121, 156, 178; Ham Common 140; Hampstead 98–9, 100, 103; Kensington 5, 23, 137, 162–3, 175, 214; Knightsbridge 155, 156, 162; Lancaster Gate 23; Maplecroft 155; St Albans 56; marriages: Judith Stott 96, 155, 157; Karin Stark 25, 168, 170, 188–9, 190, 206–8, 210, 213, 218; plays and films: *One Fine Day* 144; *A Pagan Place* 125; *Peter Pan* 24, 132; *Squeeze a Flower* 113–14; schools: Catholic University School 52; Firhouse National School 36; Keenagh National School 38; St Mary's, Rathmines 45; Terenure College 35, 49, 51, 52; smoking (Gauloises) 65, 151, 203, 204; stage shows: *Dave Allen Live* 167; *An Evening with Dave Allen* 3, 4, 143, 146,